DISCIPLES AND OTHER STRANGERS

by

Rev. Edward J. Farrell

DIMENSION BOOKS
Denville, New Jersey

DEDICATED

To Sr. Mary, Sr. Mary Frances and all the Home Visitors of Mary as they celebrate their Twenty-Fifth year of ministry to the inner City of Detroit. In gratitude for the inspiration, affection, grace I have received from them during these past ten years as their confessor.

Grateful acknowledgment is hereby made to the following for permission to print in revised and expanded form three brief sections previously published: *Review for Religious, New Catholic World, National Catholic Reporter.*

Published by

.DIMENSION BOOKS
Denville, New Jersey

Copyright © 1974 by Edward J. Farrell

CONTENTS

I DISCIPLES AND OTHER STRANGERS

> The Lord Yahweh has given me
> a disciple's tongue
> So that I may know how to
>   reply to the wearied
> he provides me with speech.
> Each morning he wakes me to hear,
> to listen like a disciple.
> The Lord Yahweh has opened my ear
>   (Isaiah 50,4).

"What is most dangerous is that which seems self-evident." Our heritage begins to disintegrate when it begins to appear self-evident, when it is no longer questioned, challenged, brought to new birth. No human or spiritual value is ever permanently won either in one's personal life or in the life of a community.

The ongoing movement of time and history is dynamic. A truth or value once attained begins almost immediately to fade and to be forgotten. The barely perceptible tides of every day wear down the mightiest rocks of inalienable truths. Everything which has its source either in man or in God must continue to be reborn, rediscovered, regenerated; otherwise it will become outmoded, useless.

What is more obvious for a Christian than "discipleship?" This is the primary experience of every believer. Is it? Certainly it was for the first Christians who asked him, "Where do you live?" and responded to his invitation, "*Come* and *see*." His final word to them was a command to "*go* and *make* disciples of all the nations." Through their response to his summons and to his teaching, the disciples were slowly transformed into apostles, witnesses and ministers. Since that time the Christian condition is almost reversed—we are born into ministry and it is *ministry which draws us into discipleship.* What a paradox! What a grace! The malaise which settled over ministry in the last few years is lifting because, true to his promise, Christ has walked by, saying to our hesitancy and our reluctance, "What do you really desire?" And in our time, we are beginning to ask, "Where do you live?", are beginning to answer his invitation, "Come and see".

In this question and in our response lies the only source of new ministry, of radical revolution, of the only Truth which makes men free. Christ wills that the fire which he came to cast upon the earth be enkindled. "You will receive power when the Holy Spirit comes on you and then you will be my witnesses. . .indeed to the ends of the earth!" (Acts 1,18). The witness to be given is what must become our reality in the midst of the confusion and chaos of our own time.

The old question of relevance was in reality the question of "power-failure," of being cut off from our roots, from our source of energy, life and truth. Many of us had been in a great glide, the momentum of the past carrying us even a little way up the new slopes of today. It was easy to be caught in the "go-go" ministry until the inevitable identity crisis. With it came the question, "Why?" and the despairing counter-question, "Is this all there is to the circus?" True ministry is rooted in faith, in discipleship. True ministry compels one to discipleship; true discipleship compels one to ministry.

> "Only faith can tell us who we are and what we should be" (Paul VI).

> "Look to Jesus who leads us in our faith and brings it to perfection" (Hebrews 12:2).

> "The most radical form of imitation is to become, like Jesus, a man of faith."

The disciple is the one who is close enough to hear and to respond to Jesus' deepest question, "Do you believe me?" (John 11,26). Everything depends upon my answer! My faith, my ministry, my life-style, my prayer, is anchored in my faith in him as present with me, "always going before me" (Matthew 28,7), "sending me" (Matthew 28,20), as the Father sent him (John 20,21). "This is the victory over the world—my faith" (John 5,4).

Inevitably our words are braver than our hearts. Have we not all experienced how difficult it is to possess deep faith? Our lack of it, our lack of power to attract, inspire and make disciples of the children of this generation—this is the world's victory over us—our lack of faith. "The Kingdom of God is not just words, it is power" (1 Cor. 4,20). And it must be the power, the faith which speaks to the world today.

Some aspects of discipleship remain constant. A certain kind of irrelevance and persecution is always a part of it, even though the irrelevance and the persecution change through the generations. What Paul wrote to the Corinthians remains true: "It seems to me God has put us apostles at the end of his parade, with the men sentenced to death; it is true we have been put on show in front of the whole universe, angels as well as men. Here we are fools for the sake of Christ, while you are the learned men in Christ; we have no power, but you are influential; you are celebrities, we are nobodies. To this day we go without food and drink and clothes; we are beaten and have no homes; we work for our living with our own hands. When we are cursed we answer with a blessing; when we are hounded, we put up with it; we are insulted and we answer politely. We are treated as the offal of the world, still to this day, the scum of the earth" (1 Cor 4,9).

These words are true not only of millieni-ums past but also of the present. They cry out to us from the tortured Third World, from the hidden and forgotten worlds of our inner cities. If the world receives us differently from the way it received Christ then we must begin to question the authenticity of our discipleship. "If the world hates you, remember that it hated me before you. If you belonged to the world, the world would love you as its own; but because you do not belong to the world, because my choice withdrew you from the world, therefore the world hates you" (John 15,18). Bonhoeffer's words ring true, "When Christ calls a man, he bids him come and die." No wonder we instinctively hesitate, are reluctant to follow, to "be-lieve" more clearly, love more deeply and follow more radically.

Faith and personal fidelity to Jesus does not come easily. Even as it did not come easily or all at once to the first disciples. Listen to and meditate carefully on the words of the four evangelists:

Mark 4,15	Do you not understand this parable? Then how will you understand any of the parables?
6,52	They were utterly and completely dumbfounded because they had not seen what the miracle of the loaves meant; their minds were closed.

7,18   Do you not understand either?

8,17   Why are you talking about having no bread? Do you not yet understand? Have you no perception? Are your minds closed? Have you 'eyes that do not see, ears that do not hear'? or do you not remember?...Are you still without perception?

9,32   But they did not understand what he said and were afraid to ask him.

10,32   They were on the road going up to Jerusalem; Jesus was walking on ahead of them; they were in a daze, and those who followed were apprehensive.

10,38   You do not know what you are asking.

16,14   He reproached them for incredulity and obstinancy, because they had refused to believe those who had seen him after he had risen!

Mark, the secretary of Peter, never forgot his own slowness in coming to believe the love and patience of Jesus. How long it took to make Peter and the others, disciples!

The Gospel of Matthew dwells specifically on what was lacking in the disciples—faith. Again and again Jesus reproaches them:

Matthew 6,30 You men of little faith (worrying about tomorrow).

8,10 I tell you solemnly, nowhere in Israel have I found faith like this (centurion).

8,26 Why are you so frightened, you men of little faith (storm at sea).

14,32 Men of little faith, why did you doubt? (Peter in the water).

17,20 Why were we unable to cast it out?...Because you have little faith...if your faith were the size of a mustard seed, you could...

Although Luke does not dwell on the disciples' slowness and lack of faith, he does drop one thunderbolt unparalleled in any of the other Gospels. He reflects the centrality of Jesus' demand for faith, posing the overwhelming question: "But when the Son of man comes, will he find any faith on earth?" It is this question which summons us to be disciples for our own time.

DISCIPLES AND OTHER STRANGERS

In John's Gospel is reflected the pattern of the thought of the synoptic Gospels—underlining the truth that discipleship is a long road and narrow, an arduous process, demanding ever deeper faith, ever more complete openness to the Spirit.

Many of Jesus' followers found the demands of discipleship too great, were unable to respond to the totality of giving which was involved.

John 6:66   After this, many of his disciples left him and stopped going with him. Then Jesus said to the twelve, "What about you, do you want to go away too?"

12,16   At the time his disciples did not understand this (entry into Jerusalem).

13,7   At the moment you do not know what I am doing but later you will understand (washing of the feet).

14,9   Have I been with you all this time...and you still do not know me? (Last Supper).

16,31   Do you believe at last?

What the first disciples discovered, what every disciple has discovered is how long it takes to believe in the truth, to believe in the love of Jesus, to experience oneself as the beloved disciple! To be a disciple is to be the beloved disciple. A disciple is chosen, to be chosen is to be loved. The Gospels make it clear that Christ chose his first disciples after spending the night before in prayer to his Father. He chose; and the disciples also chose to be his followers, responded to his call.

> You did not choose me; no, I chose you (John 15,16).

> No one can come to me unless he is drawn by the Father who sent me (John 6,44).

> I call you friends because I have made known to you everything I have learned from my Father (John 15,15).

> As the Father has loved me, so I have loved you (John 15,9).

> I have loved them as much as you loved me (John 17,23).

It is interesting that John never used the phrase "beloved disciple" of himself; it was a tribute his disciples incorporated into his Gospel because he radiated so intensely the joy of his discipleship. His Gospel makes clear that no one understood discipleship more profoundly.

What, then, is it to be a disciple? It is to experience being loved so completely that existentially we are incapable of being other than totally his. "For those who do not understand no words are possible; for those who understand no words are necessary." Even Paul stutters in his attempt to describe this experience. "Life to me is Christ" (Phil. 1,21). "I keep following, grasping ever more firmly that purpose for which Christ Jesus grasped me" (Phil. 3,13). In our own century, Charles de Foucauld cries out, "Once I believed there was a God, then I knew there was nothing else to do but live only for him."

When the experience of being disciples, of being loved so extravagantly becomes part of our deepest consciousness, it is overwhelming, even frightening. Like the prophets of old, we are hesitant, fearful. Moses responded to Yahweh's call, "But my Lord, never in my life have I been a man of eloquence either before or since you have spoken to your servant. I am a slow speaker and not able to speak well. . .If it please you, my Lord, Moses replied, send anyone you will. At this the anger of Yahweh blazed out against Moses" (Exodus 4,10). And Jeremiah: "a, a, a, Lord Yahweh, look, I do not know how to speak; I am a child! But Yahweh replied, Do not say, 'I am a child.' Go now to those to whom I send you and say whatever I command you. Do not be afraid of them, for I am with you to protect you" (Jeremiah 1,6). When Peter saw the great catch of fish, he cried out, "Leave me, Lord; for I am a sinful man. . ." But Jesus said to him, "Do not be afraid; from now on it is men you will catch" (Luke 5,8). As Yahweh promised the prophets, so Jesus promises his disciples, "Do not worry about what to speak or what to say; what you are to say will be given to you when the time comes; because it is not you who will be speaking; the Spirit of your Father will be speaking in you" (Matthew 10,19).

Although there may be anonymous Christians, there cannot be anonymous disciples. Inherent in the call to be a disciple is a call to change. No longer can one sing to himself, "I love my little world, I live serenely and safely in my private little world." He cannot be like everyone else. He can no longer ignore the question: "What am I ready to die for?" He must answer honestly, "Have I decided to become a Christian, to be a disciple?" Luke speaks uncompromising words: "When a man has had a great deal given him, a great deal will be demanded of him; when a man has had a great deal given him on trust, even more will be expected of him. I have come to bring fire to the earth and how I wish it were blazing already! There is a baptism I must still receive, and how great is my distress till it is over. Do you suppose that I am here to bring peace on earth? No, I tell you, but rather division" (Luke 12,48-51). Mark parallels this passage with, "The cup that I must drink you shall drink, and with the baptism with which I must be baptized you shall be baptized" (Mark 10,39).

For Charles de Foucauld his discipleship meant that he prayed the Word of God so constantly that it became autobiographical.

When he was murdered they found on his body a slip of paper which he had carried all his years in the desert, "Remember that you will die by violence and in pain. . .and hope that it will be today." The martyrology of the twentieth century already numbers over *one hundred million* killed and murdered in Europe. The blood of his disciples and of our brothers continues to pour out in Asia, Africa, South America.

When Malcolm Muggeridge came to a belief in Jesus, he asked all over Europe, "Where can I find the Gospel really lived?" Eventually someone told him to go to Calcutta to see Mother Teresa. There he found Someone beautiful for God. I ask myself; if I find the Gospel really lived, am I ready to live it? And "in the sound of a gentle breeze", I hear the answer, "you will find it when you are ready to live it."

To be a disciple is to breathe the Divine Milieu, to be in Christ, to be "under the influence," to hear always "Without me, you can do nothing." It is to meet every person in the Holy Spirit, in the awareness that "something more than me is what I want to give to you." What we believe becomes autobiographical, becomes a prophecy which we will fulfill. If we believe that we are "not much," we will become "not much." If we believe we are the "beloved disciples" we will become the "beloved disciples." We all desire instant success. But if we act upon even our hesitating belief, "What if it is all true?" we shall begin to reap the thirty, sixty and hundred fold promised in this life. But "Not without persecutions" (Mark 10,30).

If we do not admit to the wounds, we cannot be part of the healing. If we do not feel the bleeding wounds of our society, of the church, we are part of the sickness. To change something, we ourselves are going to be changed. If we do not change we are not a part of the healing process. To change demands boldness, passion, imagination. "The Spirit he has bestowed upon us is not one that shrinks from danger; it is a spirit of action, of love and of discipline" (II Timothy 1,7).

To be ready to live as a disciple demands a level of contemplation and discernment which may be even more than that of the cloister or the hermitage. Contemplation becomes real in conversion; conversion manifests itself in involvement. The disciple is not revitalized by working on himself but by surrendering himself to the ministry of the poor. The call to ministry and people can be ambivalent. Just as Jesus' great temptations were in terms of ministry so the temptations of the disciple may express themselves in the ministry, in people. The Spirit may push the disciple beyond the desires of his people, calling them beyond settling for less.

Conversion to discipleship means exodus. Each of us tends to become our own institution and way of life; we are easily "hooked in" to the pole of ourselves. It is easy to settle psychologically and spiritually into entrophy. We need others to help us break out of our self-addicting orbit. We need, as disciples, to breathe together, to burn together, to recognize that we are strangers in a strange land. We are aliens in a counter-culture which makes us a "surface" underground because we are disciples, because we understand, because we stand under his vision, his call.

Even as the candle or the wood cannot ignite itself, just as fire cannot sustain itself except in adhering, inhering to something, someone, so we need to be ignited, sustained by the depths of others, by their boldness, their passion, their imagination. We need the transparency of others, need others who show fidelity to the revolution. We need holy combustion, to be burning bushes which are not consumed. Only as disciples can we bring others to the inner melting point which releases the Spirit and his power. "We have received the Spirit that comes from God, to teach *us* to understand the gifts that he has given us" (I Cor. 2,13).

The call remains, "Come and see." It is not simple; nor does it take place all at once. Rather, it is evolutionary. Christ will continue to ask us to go further, and we shall not know to what lengths he will call us. "We will never go as far as when we do not know where we are going". The first disciples were not aware in the beginning that they were disciples. They had no thought of ministry. It was enough to follow him, to be with him for the rest of their lives. Growth in discipleship is to be sought, prayed for, struggled for. Discipleship becomes more and more free. The Lord will "seduce" only so far. The options become more and more clear, the temptations more and more subtle. He will ask us again and again, "What about you, do you want to go away too?" (John 6,68). Each decision to be identified with him becomes more costly—it may cost a man his life. "Enter in by the narrow gate, since the road that leads to perdition is wide and spacious and many take it; but it is a narrow gate and a hard road that leads to life, and only a few find it" (Matthew 7,13).

To be a disciple is to walk on water; yet like Paul we can be persuaded that "neither death nor life. . .nothing still to come, not any power. . .can ever come between us and the love of God made visible in Christ Jesus our Lord" (Romans 8,38).

There is no way to be a disciple except to the marrow of the bone. Otherwise we are but other strangers:

If we have died with him, then we shall live
  with him.
If we hold firm, then we shall reign with him.

21

If we disown him, then he will disown us.
We may be unfaithful, but he is
    always faithful,
for he cannot disown his own self
    (II Timothy 2,13).

II DISCIPLE: BEING CALLED
AND VOWED

"I have called you by name. You are mine. I forbid you to be afraid. I am with you" (Isaiah 43).

"With what gift shall I come into Yahweh's presence?...this is what Yahweh asks of you: only this, to act justly, to love tenderly, and to walk humbly with your God" (Mi 6,6).

"Come follow me."

"that we have heard
and we have seen with our own eyes:
that we have watched
and touched with our hands:
the Word, who is life —
What we have seen and heard
we are telling you
so that you too may be in Union with us"
(1 John 1,1).

"I call you friends, because I have made known to you everything I have learned from my Father. You did not choose me, no I chose you; and I commissioned you to go out and to bear fruit, fruit that will last."

Kadosh, Kadosh, Kadosh,
Haggios, Haggios, Haggios,
Sanctus, Sanctus, Sanctus,
Holy, Holy, Holy.

In Hebrew and Greek, in Latin and English though the word be different the reality is the same, the mystery as deep. Holy, Holy, Holy, the word of the angelic choir before the heavenly throne, is the word that comes closest to describing vowed discipleship, the laying down of one's life for Christ. It is a holy thing to hear, to follow, to bind oneself irrevocably to him, to the one who makes fidelity possible. We can be faithful because he has first vowed himself to us. "I will be with you all days."

The moment of call is dramatic, subtle, brief, as simple as that one when Jesus passed and John stared hard at him and said, "Look, there is the lamb of God. Hearing this, the two disciples followed Jesus." They followed Jesus and he knew that they were following; he did not have to hear their footsteps. He turned around to them and asked the beautiful question, "What do you want?" Touching the deepest core of their hearts, the ripple of his passing by drew them after him and they could only utter the simple question, "Where do you live?" He did not ask them, "Why do you ask?" "Come," he gently replied, "Come and see." So they went and saw and stayed with him the rest of their lives! Jesus answered their question with an imperative, a call. When Jesus calls it is not with words. As with the rich young man of Mark's Gospel, "Jesus looks steadily at him and loves him." Having experienced this loving glance of Jesus one is no longer free to be otherwise than his. A young Sister on her vow day expressed it to me in these words, "I would be sad if he did not love me enough to ask me to give him everything. He loves me; I love him. Isn't that enough." This Sister was touched and drawn by a reality far greater and more present than that which we ordinarily consider reality—the tangible everyday concrete happenings. "Love does such things."

"Who will answer?" "After that I saw a huge number, impossible to count, of people from every nation, race, tribe and language; they were standing in front of the throne and in front of the Lamb, dressed in white robes and holding palms in their hands. They shouted aloud, 'Victory to our God, who sits on the throne, and to the Lamb!...Amen. Praise and glory and wisdom and thanksgiving and honor and power and strength to our God forever and ever. Amen'" (Rev. 7,9). "Then I heard a loud voice from the throne, 'You see this city? Here God lives among men. He will make his home among them; they shall be his people, and he will be their God; his name is God-with-them'" (Rev 21,3). "Look, I am standing at the door knocking. If one of you hears me calling and opens the door, I will come in to share his meal, side by side with him" (Rev. 3,20). "I will give the hidden manna and a white stone—a

stone with a new name written on it,
known only to the man who receives it"
(Rev. 2,17).

Who will answer? The prophecy of Revelation has been fulfilled in every generation, every decade. "O God, you are my
God, I am seeking you." "I will celebrate
your love forever Yahweh, for I claim that
love is built to last forever" (Psalm 89).
These psalms have never ceased their
singing. Until the end of time there will be
those who answer, those who respond,
those who come and dare to proclaim a
vow, to say a word which will last forever.

A vow is a harvest, proclaimed and
received in great gratitude and in the
recognition that in the deepest core of our
being each one of us is God's field. In each
of us he is the sower, he is the farmer. He is
the one who has planted his field, watched
over it and cared for it.

Becoming a vowed disciple is the work
of a lifetime, a work of many people, a
work of intimate love. The realization that
the Father reaches out to men and women
and calls them, loves them so much that
they can choose no other is an awesome
experience. One almost feels compelled to
whisper. He chooses the likes of us, drawing us to himself that we might light up the
whole city. Karl Rahner expresses it so
well, "God called us at the generous age
when our weaknesses and powerlessness

were known only to him. The discovery we make little by little of our limitations and our faults is no discovery for God. It is all on our side."

For the Lord to make himself known is a long and slow process. He whispers gently into the hearts of those who are open to him a call that is humanly impossible, absurd, unhearable, yet mysteriously a call which is heard. How awesome, how holy it is to see someone stand before the altar and echo his word, his consecration, his abandonment. To vow is to follow and live the incredible risk of his abandonment into our hands so many centuries ago. He has not spoken a word since; he has not done another action. In his incredible abandonment and love he depends upon our capacity to love, our capacity to be faithful no matter what the cost, what the suffering. Only in his vow to us can we vow to him; in his fidelity is our faithfulness. "Without me you can do nothing." "Whoever believes in me will perform the same works as I do myself, he will perform even greater works" (John 14,12).

How good it is for us who have committed and vowed ourselves long ago to know that someone else hears the call we once heard, perhaps hears it even more deeply. With joy we gather around them to catch an echo, to experience the stirring of the Spirit which touches them, recognizing that they are a blessing to us, a sign and sacrament of his presence and our presence to him. It is one thing to say "yes" with words; it is another to say "yes" when one has little left to give. It is something overwhelming when one has yet everything to give and everything to lose and he answers not with a word but with the whole of his life. To vow is more than a word, it is a prophetic action, a gift of one's life, one's virginity, one's freedom, one's love. It is so holy, so humbling an experience that one wonders if he has actually done it. We need to recall again and again what has but begun in us.

Some dare to express their vows aloud before the whole community, saying by their action, "Help me to stand by my word. By myself I cannot be faithful." Their fidelity depends upon us; our fidelity depends upon theirs. They make their own words of Jesus and invite us to be what they are doing: "I am making known to you all that I have learned from my Father, and now, therefore, you are my friends, my family." They are compelled to make this love known, realizing that because he has chosen, because he has loved them, they have become free to choose him. His promise to them they now return to him, "*We* are with you." They choose him all of their lives and as a sign of his presence, they will bear fruit, not for a season but forever. What they ask of him, he will give them. The more closely they approach him the more human they become; the more they are his, the more they will belong to the community. They carry within the faith and life of the whole community our gift to him, and they become his gift to us. The vine bears fruit, the mystery of baptism, of Christian community bursts into full bloom in the vowed disciple.

It is not by accident that the word consecration is used to describe both the making of vows and the making of Eucharist. Most of the time at Eucharist we offer bread and wine, the symbol of ourselves. But on the vow day of someone close to us there is a special power and depth to the Eucharist because we see visibly the flesh and blood which we offer. The offering is human. It is a living sacrifice which we come to offer and enter into. We see his Eucharistic command, "Do this as I have done it" actualized in flesh and blood in one whom we know. We hear them promise, "This is my body given for you." "This is my blood to be shed for you." Each becomes his promise kept, a promise only he could keep, "I am with you." "I have made your name known to them and will continue to make it known, so that the love with which you loved me may be in them and so that I may be in them" (John 17,26).

Abba, my dear Father—only Jesus can say that word, only he can enable us to pray and experience that depth of relationship. Only he can close the gaps between us and bridge the distance we create. To celebrate vows is to proclaim "I *know* him in whom I believe." "I live, now not I, but Christ lives in me." To be vowed is to enter into the mystery of Jesus saying, "I am never alone, my Father is always with me". . ."the Father and I are one." Every vowed disciple carries us into deeper union with Christ. We live in a new way with each other because he has become more deeply one with us through them.

The vowed person when asked, "Who are you?" dares to answer, "I am Jesus." "I am Jesus' sister; I am Jesus' brother." "Whoever does the will of my Father in heaven, he is my brother and sister and mother" (Matthew 12,30). "My mother and my brothers are those who hear the word of God and put it into practice" (Luke 8,21). We do not know who we are. We cannot adequately say "I am" unless he says it in us. He it is who reveals the Good News of who we are and what we are for. The vowed person stands in our midst as his presence, his gift, his love. "I am Jesus for you forever, not for just a day, not only when it is convenient, not only when it is in season. I am with you because I am no longer my own. I am so totally my own that I can be yours. I have been filled. Now my life is yours, and yours, mine. Jesus lives and is alive. He is in your midst because I am yours." They have heard his words of Eucharist: "Do what I have done." "Live my life as I have lived it for you." "Love as I have loved you." "Give your life as I gave mine for you." "Abandon yourselves to them as I have to you."

The vowed disciple makes the Eucharist visible; he lives it into daily life. Kadosh, Haggios, Sanctus, Holy! Holy are those who bless us with his presence, fill us with his joy, give us a new possibility to be faithful, to be his promise kept, "I am with you always."

III DISCIPLE: DISCOVERING A KINSHIP OF GRACE

The disciple will never be alone. Jesus promised that he would not leave us orphans. "It is to the glory of my Father that you should bear much fruit, *and then you will be my disciples*" (John 15,8). He commanded us to make disciples and Jesus' command carries with it his power, his Spirit. To be a disciple is to have a *charism for community*, to experience a *kinship of grace*.

The overriding emphasis in the past few years has been in terms of the rediscovery of the person. There has been a very strong focus on self-affirmation. self-fulfillment, the self-realization which is valid and necessary but which by itself can become a false Gospel. We have seen in the past the other extreme where, in the name of community, self-denial, self-emptying, self-sacrifice became pseudo-ideals. Because of the limitations of eye span and heart span community and person have suffered much but the pain has been that of giving birth; a new wisdom has come to life. The either/or dialectic between community and person is being healed through a new depth of discernment. Reconciliation is happening because community is coming of age.

The new community is able to reflect upon its history and see that there are certain stages in its growth and development similar to the growth and development which happen in a person. There are, if you wish to use the terms, the joyful, sorrowful, glorious mysteries; or the purgative, illuminative, unitive ways; or birth, death, resurrection; Advent, Lent, Easter; child, adolescent, adult. When we are first growing up we are totally unaware of what is happening to us. This is the *hatching* stage, the *assent* phase when one can say "yes" very easily for he sees no other options. Then follows the adolescent stage, the confusion of not knowing exactly who we are, where we are, what is happening to us. This is the *dissent* and *protest* phase when one discovers his own freedom and lack of freedom. If freedom is power and authority over one's self, community is shared power and authority, the freedom of adults. Some are not yet ready for community because they do not have authority and power over themselves and therefore are not free to give power and authority over themselves to the community for the common good. This adult stage of community is an evolutionary process which is ever dynamic and never lacking in the tension which marks the human condition.

The sign of maturity, of community come of age is that it owns its own history, it believes in its future. The adult is not embarrassed over his adolescence nor at his childhood. Paul gloried in the fact of his faith. He did not apologize for being a Pharisee, or a Jew, or a sinner, a persecutor. In his last discourse Jesus gloried in all those who had been entrusted to him, "In them I am glorified" (John 17,10). "They have kept your word. . ." "I have loved them as much as you loved me. I want those you have given me to be with me where I am." We are too hesitant to affirm that our community with all its foolishness is still *our* community, *his* community.

It is essential that we be aware of the unexpressed expectations, the unconscious models by which we measure ourselves and others. It is unfair to judge the present in terms of the future, in terms of what we might someday become. Both community and person have suffered much by setting ideal goals and then judging ourselves negatively because we do not reach them. Our eyes will always see far beyond where our feet actually carry us. And we cannot altogether escape this suffering because Christ is forever calling us to a place beyond, leading us further. Whatever we do we will always be "unprofitable servants." Unless we are truly humble we will succumb to a built-in sense of inadequacy.

If a community looks at itself through old lenses or through the rear-view mirror, it may appear to be disintegrating. Seen with new lenses and perhaps from a different angle of vision, however, community may see itself converging. There is a rhythm and cycle of diffusion and convergence in community like the pulse of blood moving from the heart to the extremities and back again, a sign that the group is alive and breathing. There are moments when it seems to be in dispersion, centrifugal, everyone appears to be racing in all directions. But there is something far deeper, beyond us, beyond divergence, beyond sociology and psychology, something that holds a religious community together, something centripetal, some convergent power, centering us again and again in him.

What is this mysterious convergent power which emerges over and over when a community appears lost? What makes a community and continues to make new members, co-founders of the community? I would call it a kinship of grace given by the Holy Spirit to many diverse people, drawing them, continuing them in a particular community. Because there already exists an affinity of grace, persons are drawn to a specific community. Before they come together there exists a kinship, an emerging grace which will be mutually recognized as the kinship unfolds. At the deep root of community there is something which a number of people have in common, something beyond the general call of vocation. It is an intuitive kinship with an almost inerrant homing instinct. I am sure there are some who will psychologize this out of existence but I think this is what the Christian community means when it speaks about the *charism* of the founder and the founding members. "It takes one to catch one". . .it takes grace to recognize grace, charism to discern charism. Paul writes, "Those who are Christ's have the very scent of Christ." Dynamic and evolving like the mustard seed of the Gospel, the community charism expands and contracts, radiates and centers, producing a unitive movement, a convergence of consciousness, Chardin-like, an awareness of compatibility despite incompatibilities.

Of course there are many variables which come in to further this kinship of grace in leadership and discipleship, in ministry, in prayer. The interflow and osmosis between community and person, disciple and ministry is unfathomable. One becomes more reverent before the environment and ecology of grace. The self concept and prophetic fulfillment is much conditioned by the "community of significant persons." One would become a different person if raised in a different environment. One would be a different person in a different ecology of grace and people. Thus a person comes to a community not knowing fully who he is. Yet in some way this coming, this drawing, this kinship and response to the community charism is what leads him to discover his personal charism; he becomes more himself, more personal, more free.

In some communities there exists such a "family resemblance" in community charism that one can be mistaken for another. "Haven't I met you before?" "No, but you probably met me in my Sister." In such community there is a depth communication of grace and love, a carrying of one another in each other. All our prayers for communion cannot go unanswered. Every community has its "not yet," its incompleteness, its dark side, its rough edges which are not as inconspicuous as one would hope. Yet it is a rich compliment to a community when a member can say, "I could belong to no other community. I would not be the person I am." Such a statement indicates a keen sense of what it means to possess a deep community charism, a keen sense which tells him that he would be a different person were he in another community, that he would be diminished in some way, not able to become the total person he is meant to be.

It is not easy to be precise about community charism. Being of the Holy Spirit, it is as elusive as its Giver. Charism is not the same as one's natural talent, one's temperament, one's personality. To speak of charism is to talk about an interpersonal grace, a grace given for others, one which does not exist in isolation as the private possession of a person. It is present as a response to the action of the Spirit in one's self, as a response to a need in community, in a particular situation, in the life-history of the times.

As we have noted before, community charisms are not static. They are incarnational and situational, developmental, changing, growing, increasing, waning. In this way they are similar to prophetic graces, impermanent and reversible. They appear to be given for a particular need at a particular time. Some are leaves which last but a season; others are mighty branches grafted into the vine, continuing for centuries. Charisms are deeper identifications with Christ, more often the suffering and redemptive Christ. Charisms for community are costly. There is an intuitive hesitancy, reluctance, resistance in the one who bears the charism. Most often it is the least likely member who is chosen to carry the full charism of the community. The Spirit can be quenched, the fire can be left unfed, a community can conspire against itself. Efficacious charisms, which have to work independently of the persons and community to whom they have been given, do not exist. Charisms wither and die; only the shell, the fossil remain. It takes a whole community to sustain its charism, as history shows so well. How often a community did not measure up to its charism and the Gospel ceased to be heard in a particular time, in a particular place.

Time, place, culture shape and condition every person and thus every community. After ten years we remain the same person but often the differences far outweigh the resemblances. At certain critical moments a person, a community can make a "quantum leap," a self-transcendence, a radical conversion to a new level of life and consciousness. Crisis can generate greatness. "Where sin abounds, grace more abounds."

A charism like a talent can complete and perfect itself, then find it can go no further. An artist reaches a certain point of excellence but if he is to go further he must let go of what he has accomplished thus far, forget the familiar technique which he has developed and begin over in a new direction. The law of charism and grace is that one must die in order to bring forth new life. This runs counter to our natural desire for stability, security, to our tendency to absolutize something once and for all. To live on pilgrimage is not to our liking. We find it difficult to fold our tents again and again as the Spirit moves, draws us beyond our natural pace.

Each one owns something of the charism of the community; no one, however, has the totality. Only in communion with one another can the full charism be discerned and developed. Each member sincerely believes, desires Jesus as his center. At the same time each must humbly admit that *his* center is not yet *Jesus'* center. He has something of Jesus, he has something of the Spirit but he is not yet Jesus' center. No one of us will ever be his center; we grope our way towards this by recognizing our common need to allow him to center us in himself. He alone can shape our clay into wholeness, into community. We remain on the potter's wheel never quite finished, in a growing awareness that if we remove ourselves from his guiding hands we will fly in all directions, if we fail to respond to the touch of his creative Spirit, we will spin lopsided, formless.

The Spirit alone breathes cohesiveness into a community. He alone can sustain the differences tolerated within a community; only in the depth of his love can a community remain intact. The discerning Spirit leads us beyond the ventilation of feelings, beyond the articulation of positions to the realm, the gift of understanding. "I can know only what I have said when you tell me what you understand." That we might come to such understanding he gives the deeper gift of "tongues," the gift of interpreting the private language of each, the silences of each. It is more than a matter of knowing, accepting diversity, it involves the ability to be open, to expand enough to welcome the diversity as gift. Each becomes the diversity of the other in a way which allows the diversity to become part of the unity. To receive the charism of the community is to become the corporate person of the community. To come to know one member, is to come to know something of the whole. The family resemblance is inescapable. One no longer simply gives one's self, but he gives something of the wholeness of the community, something of the wholeness of Christ. For Christ never lets go of his disciples and those who through their words believe in him. As the *Fourth Eucharistic Prayer* says, "Even when we lose your friendship, you again and again offer a covenant to us." Far from being divisive, differences should be an enriching factor within community, the deepest gift we can give to one another. Were we all alike, no communication would be possible; there would be no gift to give, no gratitude to express.

He always loves those who are his own in the world and he continues to show the depth of his love (Fourth Eucharistic Prayer). He renews his covenant through Eucharist and the daily bread of community. Each person in community comes from him and is in some way his covenant with us, his promise kept. We are indeed extraordinary ministers of the Eucharist to one another. The Spirit in one activates the Spirit in the other even though it is not always the Holy Spirit who is activated.

The charism of and for community, the kinship of grace, is distinctive and unique. There exists a *bondedness* which does not yield to description nor to definition. It is simply there, deeply felt, ever creative, like the distinctiveness of one's own family spirit. It does not admit of comparison or of qualitative judgment. It is a difference which makes all the difference. A community charism is an identity, an identification; no other is possible. For those who have it, no explanation is necessary; for those who do not, no explanation is intelligible. Community charism involves a mystery. "You have not chosen Me." (We have not chosen each other). "I have chosen you." What a humble mystery it is, to have been chosen by him, to have been drawn together by him in order to discover him in and through one another for the rest of one's life!

The charism of Community is interwoven, inseparable from the charism of ministry. Both interact, mutually support, validate, enrich one another. Our consecration to him can happen only through our consecration to one another. Each one of his invitations to "Come" involves the command to "Go,"—a going, however, which far from separating one from community, only serves to deepen one's roots.

Christian community is the new frontier. The charism of community, the mysterious kinship of grace is an ocean inviting limitless exploration. The interdependence of the charisms of ministry and community is ripening into a new consciousness releasing great spiritual creativity.

Since no *one* possesses the fullness of the charism of community, community no longer exists by legislation; its life is sustained through the kinship of grace. Realistically considered, community admits that there is as much or as little community as the members desire, and that there can be no change, no growth except in and through the personal decisions of its members, that it is the saints alone who have the capacity to create, to move a community. Each has the power to affect his community in proportion to his personal wholeness, his holiness, his love, his capacity to draw down the Spirit into his community. Needed today are those who, like the Buddhist Monk, ignite themselves as a sign to their followers. Each disciple is called to make immolation for the new life of his community. Each disciple must be an intercessor, a mediator in the Pauline sense of making up in himself what is lacking in the corporate body, a victim in the deepest sense for his brothers and sisters.

IV DISCIPLE: CREATING A COMMUNITY OF FRIENDS

> Let them cultivate the art of praise in dealing with one another and with those they serve. Let them freely and sincerely express their esteem for one another, their gratitude and respect. Let them not withhold from one another, and especially from their sister, what the heart tells them should be hers.

> Covenant: Sisters of Providence
> Terre Haute, Indiana

If a community is not a family of friends, then it is not a Christian community. Community like a family does not simply "happen" all of a sudden. Co-existence, external identity in residence, meals, dress will not create a family of friends. Community is built consciously, deliberately, worked at day by day, chosen again and again. Far easier begun than maintained and developed, community growth demands struggle, suffering. Experience shows that confrontation in anger comes more instinctively than affirmation in love; thus the creation of a community demands time, deliberate openness, patience with the slow process of discovery and appreciation. The most obvious effect of original and cumulative sin is our emotional, psychic, spiritual isolation and insulation from one another. In each one of us there is ingrained a deep fear which rises out of our love, our need for one another. We fear that our love, our need will not be reciprocated. The words of John's Epistle humble us. "In love there can be no fear, but fear is driven out by perfect love; because to fear is to expect the worst and anyone who is afraid is still imperfect in love" (1 John 4,18). Who of us can claim a fearlessness; who would dare to claim perfect love? We love as we *can* love at the moment, not as we are called to love, not as someday we will be able to love. God alone can love perfectly without fear. As Philip Neri prayed to Christ, so are we tempted to say to one another, "Beware of me, lest I betray you."

The first step in the long journey into community is to pose the question, "How do I want to be loved?" It is the most basic question of the human person. Each must take the time to bring the implicit into personal expression. How do I want to be loved?

> I want to be loved totally, extravagantly, passionately, deeply, intensely, faithfully, without end. At the same time I want to be worthy of such love. I do not want to be loved for nothing. I want to be loved reciprocally. I want to be able to return the love given to me.
>
> I do not want to be loved exclusively nor in isolation. I want everyone to be loved with the same fullness. I want this love to be generative, creative, reaching beyond myself.

And in this very effort to describe how I want to be loved, I discover how I must love. The first step in celebrating another is the celebration of one's self and a long time passes in this discovery. How long it took as an infant to know our own hands and feet, to discover that they were a part of us. If this be true then how much more time is required to discover that truth expressed by Unamuno, "My neighbor is my unknown self."

If we look closely at our own life, we are amazed to recognize how little time we spend on a personal level with the people who are most in our daily life. I needed a summer in group work to discover this gap in myself. The work involved presence to one another eight hours a day, five days a week for a month. There was no agenda but that of our presence to one another. I do not believe that I had ever before spent an uninterrupted eight hours with my Father, Mother, brother or sisters. What a revelation to discover how much time I had invested in things and actions, how little time and life I had "wasted" on people.

Wisdom begins when one at last experiences that the ultimate charism is love. Only love reveals the truth within another person. Man's greatest achievement lies not in art, nor in science, politics, economics but in the realm of human friendship. There is no other human power. Friendship does not rest on education culture, talent, inheritance but solely in the human heart. And perhaps the most human experience of love lies in the awesome discovery of one's self in another, a friend who is one's other self. "Love knows of no devotion greater than to be shore to the ocean."

The miracles and healings of the Gospel are intended for each one of us, for who of us is not blind, deaf, dumb, crippled, leperous when it comes to the practice of friendship. We need new eyes, new ears, tongues, hands and feet in all our dealings with one another. We need to see, to hear with the eyes and the ears of Christ. What an experience it must have been to meet the glance of Jesus! "Jesus looked steadily at him and loved him" (Mark 10,21). Even had the rich young man not been rich up until that moment, he was forever after. Imagine Zacchaeus in his sycamore tree when Jesus looked up and spoke to him, "Zacchaeus, come down. Hurry, I must be your guest today" (Luke 19,1). Remember Nathaniel's total act of faith and discipleship when Jesus looked at him and said "I saw you under the fig tree" (John 2,49).

The theme of community, the secret and mysteries of the human heart are discovered and explored over and again in the parables, the parables of the kingdom in Matthew's Gospel, the parables of forgiveness in Luke's Gospel. Perhaps my favorite commentary on the Parable of the Ten Lepers is in the story of Martin Bell, "Where are the Nine?" His insight is so lucid. "Condemnation is easier than investigation. If we take the time to investigate the reasons why people act as they do, we would find that they have to act the way they do, and that such action in the light of the circumstances is quite understandable and totally forgivable and even completely reasonable and just as it should be." Whatever a person does is intelligible, purposeful to himself so one must listen to that subjective world of the other. No one asks for the judgment of another; each one hopes for understanding, that understanding which is the only bridge to another person. As the New Testament scripture scholar, John Robinson, once stated, "The kingdom of heaven is not only *within* you but *between* you!"

A second step in the creation of a community into a family of friends is to express one's positive perceptions of another. A simple process similar to the following might be used: Begin with three questions: What do you like and admire about this person? What would you like to give of yourslef to this person? What would you like to receive or need from this person? This exercise is best done in small groups of no more than six or eight people. Each is asked to write out his response using a separate sheet of paper for each person. Each is also asked to answer these same questions about himself, writing out his own response. Each is urged to be as specific and honest as possible, although poetic imagination and description are encouraged. People can be described through the medium of various things: flowers — rose/daisy; water — spring/fountain; animals — butterfly/elephant; music — flute/cello; color — dawn lavender/twilight blue; precious stone — ivory/emerald; texture — corduroy/satin, etc.

This exercise is intended to be an exercise in prayer, of entering into the presence of another in reverence and love. It should begin with prayer, continue through prayer and conclude in prayer. When everyone has finished writing out his responses to the three questions, the group comes together to hear what each one has written. Starting at random with anyone in the group, that person listens to what each has written about him, then last of all expresses what he has written about himself. If it is difficult to express what you like about another person, what you would like to give to him, what you would like to receive, it is far more difficult to listen to others speak well of you. You begin to discover that each person sees you in a unique way, listens to you differently. Each one mirrors you originally, "reads," says your name as it has never been said before.

Every person is a world globe with 360° circumference. There are but a few degrees of our surface, latitude and longitude, which any one person can grasp. And this is on the outside. Most of what happens in us cannot be sensed on an external level. It takes a whole community to encompass another person. What a joy it is to discover the beautiful sensitivity which people have for one another! How much we have to learn from one another, how much we need to grow in one another. How much we miss in each person, how much we never see or hear or appreciate in those closest to us. How long it takes for the beauty, the suffering, the secret good, the mysterious depth of another to dawn upon our consciousness.

It is embarrassing to hear the unique, original appreciation and insight another has for you. Few ever verbalize such thoughts before the funeral eulogy. We need to experience more embarrassing moments in which friends celebrate one another in the beautiful virtue of admiration. This should be a frequent prayer, the grace to discover more and more of one another's gift and talent. It is a grace but at the same time a grace dependent upon the natural quality of letting one's self be known. Too many believe too little in themselves, see too little of themselves. One of the richest ways of allowing ourself to be known is to express our awareness and admiration of another. Each one of us has a special capacity to help another discover the colors of his rainbow.

One of the more neglected of our human endowments is our capacity to remember, to take delight in our past which becomes present by our recall. It is good to remember how we have deposited ourselves, how the Lord "writes straight with crooked lines," to think of all the footprints, handprints, word prints, heart prints, love prints which have been deposited in others, which have been imprinted upon oneself. We are each a breathing mosaic of people. Continually we give something of ourselves to others, receiving something of them into ourselves. Continually we are being created, formed, consciously and unconsciously, lovingly and unlovingly. Our very presence is creative or contracting.

> In your most frail gesture are things which
>   enclose me,
> or which i cannot touch because they are
>   too near
> your slightest look easily will unclose me
> though i have closed myself as fingers,
> you open always petal by petal myself as
>   Spring opens
> (touching skilfully, mysteriously) her
>   first rose.

> (e. e. cummings)

Each person sends out his own signals, vibrations, radiation. Each one creates his own environment and atmosphere. We can give much or give little. We can absorb much or little. We can reflect much or little.

There are depths of presence and communion open to us. One can go down deep into the presence of another where there is no sound, no words. An immense or brief amount of time is needed to interpenetrate another, to be with him in his center, his holy of holies. There are Grand Canyons, Rocky mountains, oceans, deserts, oases to be discovered in each person, in oneself. In myself I find my joys, my peace, my love, but also I find my fears, my desert, my sin, my non-belief, my lie. There are times when I do not believe in me, then I need you to believe in me; times when I do not love myself, then I need you to love me. There are times when I am in a state of emptiness, meaninglessness; I just need Someone's presence.

A group of friends, a fraternity is a gift. There are times when we must be compelled to discover our better self, times when this can happen only in the group situation. I have difficulty communicating with a particular person. Alone we could never bridge the gap between us, but in the group setting we are enabled to come to some understanding. Our Lord pointed us in this direction when he asked his disciples, "What do you think of me?" "Who do you say that I am?" He asks this of all of us. He was not having an identity crisis; he knew who he was. It is we who do not know who we are. Only by coming to know him can we come to know ourselves. He asks that other question, "Do you love me?" Again he does not need to know; it is we who need to know if we love, if we are generative, creative of ourselves, of one another.

This exercise is but a step in a direction, inviting each to own one's community, to be a co-creator of the environment, the human ecology where we have to live, breathe and grow. It is not a simple short-cut. It is not a game or an artificial sensitivity session. If one must name it, let it be called Spiritivity. It is the beginning of a process, a "priming" of that which is already there but which needs to be set flowing.

One cannot simply "belong" to a community any longer. There are no passive members for if one is not a co-founder one soon becomes a *con*founder of the community. It is not enough for a community to be founded once upon a time. Every community gets lost, wanders into error and sin, as do its members. No community is ever more than its component persons. Every community has to be found again and again as the lost sheep. Everything human has to be born again; every generation needs metanoia. This is the secret fountain of youth: Christ who is always new calling us to new life, new community, a new family of friends.

Only Jesus makes community possible! Only his love can bring together what sin puts asunder. Community is always sacrificial; its price is in the laying down of one's life, one's own way, one's own will. Otherwise, the "miracle of dialogue" all too soon becomes the *illusion* of dialogue. Ministry outside the community is far easier, more "rewarding" than ministry at home. The ministry of words and activity is less demanding than the ministry of shared life and presence. The best of oneself is for export; the hole in the doughnut is left for the home community. Yet the Holy Spirit is at all times "bent" over the human "Body of Christ," the Church, "with ah! bright wings." The stirrings of discipleship are clearly evident today. The community of disciples has more than awakened to new depths. When the history of the Church in our times is written, perhaps the most significant revolution will have been the rediscovery of ministry within community, the ministry of disciples to one another, the prophetic expectation, the courage and joy to believe, hope and love one another in his name and power.

Loving people means summoning them forth
   with the loudest and most insistent of calls;
it means stirring up in them
   a mute and hidden being
     who can't help leaping at the sound of
      our voices—
a being so new
     that even those who carried him
     didn't know him,
   and yet so authentic
     that they can't fail to recognize him
     once they discover him.
All love includes fatherhood and motherhood.
   To love someone is to bid him to live,
     invite him to grow.

Since people don't have the courage to mature
    unless someone has faith in them,
  we have to reach those we meet
      at the level where they stopped developing,
        where they were given up as hopeless,
            and so withdrew into themselves
            and began to secrete
              a protective shell
          because they thought they were alone
            and no one cared.
They have to feel they're loved very deeply
        and very boldly
  before they dare appear humble and kind,
          affectionate, sincere
            and vulnerable.
            —from Louis Evely's *That Man Is You*

The mission and life of the church will always be the continual formation of community. "Christ wants us to manifest, by living together in spite of difficulties involved, that his love and his Spirit are stronger than all the forces of disruption. . .to manifest that the liberation of man is already begun" (O.M.I. Chapter). At the root of community and fraternity is abandonment to kenosis, the spiritual poverty of Christ, the desire to share our lives with one another as Christ shares his life with us. In the "bread line" of the daily Eucharist we receive his capacity to dare to utter his words to one another—this is my body given for you; this is my blood to be shed for you.

V DISCIPLE: FASTING IN BODY, HUNGERING IN SPIRIT

"He fasted for forty days and forty nights, after which he was hungry" (Mt. 4,2).

"But the time will come, the time for the bridegroom to be taken away from them; that will be the time when they will fast" (Luke 5,35).

"But when you fast, put oil on your head and wash your face so that no one will know you are fasting except your Father who sees all that is done in secret; and your Father who sees all that is done in secret will reward you" (Mt. 6,17).

"So it was that after fasting and prayer they laid their hands on them and sent them off" (Acts 13,3).

"For three days he (Paul) was without his sight and took neither food nor drink" (Acts 9,9).

In his Letter to the Holy Year Committee (May 31, 1973) Paul VI wrote "We trust that the value of penitential practices will be rediscovered, as a sign and way of grace, as a commitment for the deep renewal which receives its full efficacy in the sacrament of penance." How much needs to be rediscovered! The Eucharistic

Fast from midnight which had been observed since the fourth century was ended by Pius XII January 6, 1953 because of the social and economic changes of modern society. In the apostolic constitution *Poenitemini* of Paul VI, February 17, 1966 there was a total reorganization of ecclesiastical discipline with regard to fasting and abstinence which soon led to dispensation entirely from fast and abstinence except on Ash Wednesday and Good Friday.

It is amazing how easily we shed the traditional fasting practices and totally forget them! And very little seems to have replaced them. In our overfed society there is much weight-watching and diet-cola-ing but these have little to do with fasting. Fasting is an intentional abstention from food on *religious* grounds; it is an essential act of the religious soul. Almost everywhere and at all times fasting has held a place of great importance since it is closely linked with the intimate sense of religion. Perhaps this is the explanation for the demise of fasting in our day. When the sense of God diminishes fasting disappears. Perhaps more accurately, when the vision fades, i.e. the wisdom, language and tradition are no longer understood, the habit and practice wither away.

Fasting seems to be one of those religious values forever being forgotten; lost, yet having a marvelous resiliency and life-span coextensive with humanity itself. What the parents throw away as useless, the children bring back as new-found treasures. What one generation discards the next generation unearths and enshrines.

The ghost of Ghandi hovers over our generation. His fasting reopens a forgotten page of the Gospel. As the patron saint of the peace movement his life style has breathed his spirit into many. Hinduism and Buddhism in their American varieties have awakened and stirred a long-buried religious intuition. Who can forget the haunting words of Hermann Hesse's *Siddhartha* when asked what he could do after spending three years with the holy men in the forest, "I can think, I can fast, I can wait." Perhaps certain generations have to recapitulate and re-experience the cumulative spiritual wisdom of the race. Ours seems to be that kind of a generation. We do not know where to go until we understand our roots. Our cultural and spiritual impasse, as we thrust our head out amid the stars, sends vibrations back to the tips of our toes. The fences have all come tumbling down, our unlimited and unlimitable freedoms create a nervous insecurity. So man looks into his inner resources, his unused power, his hidden self. The consumer society generates its antithesis; the man who stands against the conditioned reflex, the man who is free not to consume, the man who can fast.

The man who fasts stands in a noble tradition. In the religious experience of mankind, fasting has been a prelude and means to a higher spiritual life. Man disturbs and destroys the inner order of spirit and body if he fails to control the amount he eats and drinks. Fasting in the not-so-primitive religions was related to death and rebirth, to a period of quiessence which appears to represent the state of non-existence preceding conception. All activities are suspended as far as possible. Fasting precedes the rebirth of nature, sowing, harvesting—a practice echoed in our old ember days.

One of the most powerful motives for fasting in antiquity was the fear of demons who gained power over men through eating and in this way entered their bodies. Could this be related to Genesis and Adam's temptation? In an ancient and popular document, "Testament of Adam," the first hour of the night was the time for adoration of the demons during which time the demons ceased to do evil and harm men. So the hour after sunset was the hour of freedom to end one's fast without fear. There is a startling association between Adam's disobedience in eating and our redemption in the eating and drinking of the Body and Blood of Christ.

> "of the tree of the knowledge of good and evil you are not to eat, for on the day you eat of it you shall most surely die" (Gen. 2,17).

> "If you do not eat the flesh of the Son of Man and drink his blood, you will not have life in you" (Jn 6,53).

In all world religions fasting is recognized as a preparation for communion/intercourse with the deity and for the reception of ecstatic or magical powers. Abstinence from food and drink induced a state of susceptibility to visions and dreams in which direct access to the realities of the spiritual world could be found. Fasting makes one fit for union with the Divine. In many rites the neophytes fasted before receiving the mixed sacramental drink. Abstention made one receptive to ecstatic revelations. Moses and Daniel both fasted in preparation for the reception of divine revelation.

In the Old Testament fasting appears to be an act of self-renunciation and self-discipline which is designed to make an impression on God. Privation of nourishment, of anything agreeable to the senses seemed to be the ideal means of expressing one's dependence upon God. Fasting expressed mourning, going without a meal which is an occasion and expression of joy. It expressed the desire to heal the sick, to ask for spiritual guidance. It was an appeal for divine mercy, for forgiveness and conversion. It manifested penitence and the will for atonement.

True fasting which leads to salvation is a real bowing of the person in moral action, in loving service to the poor and unfortunate among the people. Fasting signals a conversion of heart, an orientation to love. It can be a radical turning of man towards

God and his commandments, especially love of one's neighbor. "Man must through fasting dispose himself even materially to allowing his neighbor to share his property in spite of the claims of self-love" (Paul VI). The worth of fasting, as of any other act, lies in the faith and love of which it is the expression. Without such faith and love it is meaningless.

In the New Testament fasting continued and was surpassed. It pointed toward participation in the pascal mystery of Christ and a striving toward his return. Fasting in itself, like any external human act, is ambivalent. It can be spiritually dangerous in that it tends to become a material achievement performed to one's own advantage. So Jeremiah could utter, "When they fast, I will not hear them" (Jer 14,12). Our Lord warned his disciples, "When you fast do not put on a gloomy look as the hypocrites do: they pull long faces to let men know they are fasting. I tell you solemnly, they have had their reward" (Mt 6,16).

Jesus when asked refused to lay down any specific regulations on the nature and frequency of fasting for his disciples. This was a shock and a scandal even to John's disciples. But the presence of the kingdom dawning and breaking into human history in Jesus' presence and ministry was the occasion for joy and thanksgiving. "But the time will come for the bridegroom to be taken away from them, and then they shall fast" (Mt. 9,16). The teaching of Jesus on fasting is new and distinctive by omission and by the absence of almost any accent upon it. "Fast. . .so that no one will know you are fasting except your Father who sees all that is done in secret" (Mt. 6,17). Fasting is service of God. It is a sign and symbol of the conversion to God which takes place in secret. This conversion to the Father has the intimacy of the nuptial mystery; therefore fasting from now on has to be in secret. Fasting before God, the Father of those who turn to him, is *joy*. There is no room for melancholy signs of mourning. The sign of Christian fasting is to be joy and charity; Jesus is bringing new wine; a total transformation is happening. Fasting is no longer the self-renunciation and self-discipline arduously forged by the human will, designed to make an impression on God. Now, fasting is an aftermath, a reflex consequence of living in Christ and having Christ in oneself.

> All I want is to know Christ and the power of his resurrection and to share his sufferings by reproducing the pattern of his death (Phil. 3,10).

> I treat my body hard and make it obey me (1 Cor. 9,27).

> All the athletes at the games go into strict training: they do this just to win a wreath that will wither away, but we do it for a wreath that will never wither. That is how I run, intent on winning; that is how I fight, not beating the air (1 Cor. 9,25).

You cannot belong to Christ Jesus unless you crucify all self-indulgent passions and desires (Gal. 5,24).

If in union with Christ we have imitated his death, we shall also imitate him in his resurrection. We must realize that our former selves have been crucified with him to destroy this sinful body and to free us from the slavery of sin. . .and in that way you too must consider yourselves to be dead to sin but alive for God in Christ Jesus (Rom. 6,5).

That is why you must not let sin reign in your mortal bodies or command your obedience to bodily passions, why you must not let any part of your body turn into an unholy weapon fighting on the side of sin: you should instead offer yourselves to God, and consider yourselves dead men brought back to life; you should make every part of your body into a weapon fighting on the side of God, and then sin will no longer dominate your life, since you are living by grace and not by law (Rom. 6,12).

As a Christian I may do anything but that does not mean that everything is good for me. I may do everything but I must not let anything dominate me. Food was meant for the stomach and the stomach for food: but God has no permanent purpose for either. But you cannot say that our physical body was made for sex indulgence; it was made for God, and God is the answer to our deepest longings. . .Have you realized the almost incredible fact that your bodies are integral parts of Christ himself?. . .You are not your own property; you have been bought and paid for. That is why you should use your body for the glory of God (1 Cor. 6,12).

He was bearing our faults in his own body on the cross, so that we might die to our faults and live for holiness; through his wounds you have been healed (1 Pet. 2,24).

Try then to imitate God as children of his that he loves and follow Christ by loving as he loved you, and which he perfectly expressed when he gave himself up for us in sacrifice to God (Eph. 5,1).

You will look for me (Jn. 13,33).

I urge you, my dear people, while you are visitors and pilgrims, to keep yoursleves free from the selfish passions that attack the soul (1 Pet. 2,11).

That is why you must kill everything in you that belongs only to earthly life. . .You have stripped off your old behavior with your old self, and you have put on a new self which will progress towards true knowledge the more it is renewed in the image of its creator (Col. 3,5).

Let me put it like this: if you are guided by the Spirit you will be in no danger of yielding to self-indulgence, since self-indulgence is the opposite of the Spirit, the Spirit is totally against such a thing, and it is precisely because the two are so opposed that you do not always carry out your good intentions (Gal. 5,16).

You must give up your old way of life: you must put aside your old self, which gets corrupted by following illusory desires. Your mind must be renewed by a spiritual revolution, so that you can put on the new self that has been created in God's way, in the goodness and holiness of the truth (Eph. 4,22).

Forget about satisfying your bodies with all their cravings (Rom. 13,14).

I have told you often and I repeat it today with tears, there are many who are behaving as the enemies of the cross of Christ. They are destined to be lost. They make food into their god and they are proudest of something they ought to think shameful (3 Phil. 16).

Our Lord's disciples asked him why they were unable to cast out the epileptic demoniac of Mark 9. "This is the kind," he answered, "that can only be driven out by prayer and *fasting.*" This "and fasting" is not found in all the early texts, but it is not without significance that it was added and retained by the early Christian communities.

These words of Scripture are unequivocal and sobering. They are an invitation, a command; a judgment, a consolation. Each one hears these words at different moments in his life with Jesus. The way is long; we would be easily disheartened did we not know that he travels with us. His holy people light the way for us again and again. Fasting was an integral part of their lives and of their rule. It was seen as an integration of the body into the whole life of faith. It became a spiritual sacrifice, greater than alms for it involved the body, not just money. It made concrete and real spiritual fasting, that offering to God of the sacrifice of a humble and contrite heart. St. Jerome writes, "Without Ceres and Bacchus, Venus becomes cold," i.e. without banqueting and wining, concupiscence of the flesh is lessened. Augustine preached: "Don't believe that fasting suffices. Fasting punishes you, but it will not restore your brother! Your privations will be fruitful if you provide for the needs of another. Certainly you have deprived your body, but to whom did you give that which you deprived yourself? What did you do with the things you denied yourself? How many poor people could be nourished by the meal which you did not take today? Fast, then, in such a way that when another has eaten in your place you may rejoice in the meal you have taken. Then your offering will be received by God."

For the early Christians "going without meat" was "enabling our neighbor to eat." About the year 128 Aristides, a journalist, explained to the Emperor Hadrian, the manner in which Christians lived: "When someone is poor among them, who has need of help, they fast for two or three days, and they have the custom of sending him the food which they had prepared for themselves."

St. Benedict's rule of the Sixth century is no less meaningful and vibrant in the Twentieth century: "In your every meal let the strict meaning of the words apply. Let each one, over and above the measure prescribed for him, offer something to God of his own free will *in the joy of the Holy Spirit.* That is to say, let him stint himself of food. . .From his body he may withhold some food, drink, sleep, talking and jesting; and with the joy of spiritual desire he may look forward to Holy Easter" (Chapt. 49).

St. Bernard in the Twelfth century wrote, "If the mouth alone be guilty, it alone should fast, but if the other members have sinned, why should they not fast."

In 1950 Pius XII spoke in these words: "What he has rescued from vanity the faithful Christian will give to charity and thus mercifully provide for the Church of the poor. This was the practice in the primitive church. By fasting and abstaining from things that were perfectly permissible, they supplied the sources of charity."

Paul VI in the Apostolic Constitution "Poenitemini" of February 17, 1966 reminded the Christian people:

All its members are called to participate in the work of Christ and therefore to participate also in his expiation.

Penitence, required by the inner life, confirmed by the religious experience of mankind, and in the object of a particular precept of divine revelation assumes "in

Christ and the Church" new dimensions infinitely broader and more profound.

Following the Master, every Christian must renounce himself, take up his own cross and participate in the sufferings of Christ.

Little acts of penitence. . .become a form of participation in a special way in the infinite expiation of Christ.

The task of bearing in his body and soul the death of the Lord affects the whole life of the baptized person at every instant and in every aspect.

The duty of doing penance is motivated above all by participation in the sufferings of Christ.

"Do penance"—imperatives too often repeated are no longer heard. The era of the imposed fast is but a memory now. Fasting today is an exercise of freedom, of spiritual exploration, of creative love and identity with the poor. The example and inspiration of others is always contagious. The Muslim world is scandalized by the absence of fasting among Christians. In Algeria, especially, the corporate fast of Ramadan is strictly observed. In the Muslim calendar Ramadan is the ninth lunar month. The fast consists in complete abstention from food and drink, tobacco and perfumes and sexual intercourse from sunrise to sunset of each day. Exemption from the fast, becasue of temporary disability, must be made up later on. This fasting experience of a whole nation is a deep witness to the solidarity of the people in their faith and tradition.

The primitive natives of Venezuela have a natural intuition of the necessity to sacrifice the body to something more interior. Fasting for them is a sign of manliness—that their spirit is stronger than any appetite. "They are less materialistic than we are," remarked a Little Brother of Jesus who had lived among them for eight years.

The Mormons have an admirable tradition of fasting on the first Sunday of the month, from the evening meal of Saturday to the evening meal of Sunday, in order to devote themselves more effectively to prayer, reflection and charity.

In my retreat work for the past eight years I have asked retreatants to make a "desert day" each week, to fast from sunrise to sunset. Most of them have never experienced a full day of fast and find it to be an extraordinary day of prayer and grace. The age of participants has ranged from those in their teens to others in their seventies or eighties.

When I spent my month in the desert, it came as a great shock that I, who had never been hungry before, could actually starve to death! Never before had I experienced my utter physical dependence upon the Father to give me this day my daily bread! Never had I heard so deeply his words over his body and blood—"Take and eat," "Take and drink."

There is a deep correlation and connection between the fast of the body and the hunger of the soul/spirit. The body fast has a special way of sensitizing the soul/spirit, the soul/spirit has a way of enabling the body to transcend itself. Eating can be self-preoccupying and compulsive, diminishing our presence and consciousness to others and to the world. Fasting can be a good barometer of the range of our consciousness. When something or someone greater is present, we forget food. Lovers grow thin! Fasting is a sign of someone, something greater in our psychic center and consciousness. It uncovers our hidden capacities for greater strength, greater freedom. I know of a priest who fasts before anointing the sick so that the strength which is received through the fast may be given to the one anointed. Mutual fasting before the celebration of the Sacrament of Penance is an ancient tradition. Fasting was the most common prelude to sacrament, sacrifice and consecration. Each of the vows is a life-long fast. Vowing is possible only because Christ's presence in one is greater than are any of the values offered in sacrifice. Fasting creates room within, enabling Christ to fill us with his hunger, his thirst.

He hungers, thirsts in hundreds of millions day after day who cry out to us, "Give us this day our daily prayer in the name of our common Father." Paul VI has admonished repeatedly, "Nations who enjoy economic plenty have a duty of self-denial, combined with an active proof of love towards our brothers who are tormented by poverty and hunger."

Not easily forgotten is the witness of Simone Weil, the young Jewish philosopher, who died of starvation in 1943 at the age of thirty-three. Being prevented from exposing herself to the dangers which then hung over the lives of her Jewish compatriots in the concentration camps, she desired at least to share their privations, strictly keeping to rations which never exceeded the amounts allocated to those in the camps. As a consequence she starved to death. She felt at ease only when she was on the lowest rung of the social ladder, lost among the masses of the poor, the outcasts of this world. In her writing the following was found: "God consented through love to cease to be everything so that we might be something; we must consent through love to cease to be anything so that God may become everything again." May each of us learn to eat our hunger and drink our thirst in the power of his hidden presence in us.

> He made these forty days
> a holy season of self-denial
> by fasting from earthly food.
> By his victory over the tempter
> he has taught us to overcome
> the hidden corruption of evil
> and so share his paschal meal
> in purity of heart,
> until we celebrate its fulfillment
> in the promised land of heaven.
>
> *Preface* – First Sunday of Lent.

71

VI DISCIPLE: I. PRAYING IN JESUS

I pray. I pray much. I have spent more time in prayer than in anything else in my life. What I would be without prayer, I cannot imagine. I do not know what to say when someone tells me, "I've given it up." These words strike me dumb. I want to be able to say something, to reach out to heal the anguish and hurt which I feel in those words. When someone tells me that he experiences nothing of my joy or peace or love I feel terribly poor, powerless, guilty and I am driven to pray even more because I do not know what to do or to say. There is no place to go but to him and to plead, "They have no wine."

Today there are many who "sit in darkness and the shadow of death," many who weep hopelessly: "I have no home." "I have no father," "no mother," "no brother," "no sister." "I do not believe." "I do not hope." "I do not love." I am uncomfortable with these cries even as I feel guilty with the blind, the deaf, the crippled, the retarded. I feel guilty because I have done so little with so much and my shoulders sag under the burden.

I find it more and more difficult to speak or to write about prayer because actually I know only my own prayer and my own prayer is simply who I am. It is who I am at the deepest and truest moment of presence to myself and to all that I am—people, world, Jesus. It is a breaking into the depths of something beyond words and experience; not an experience with symbols and psychedelic colors but with dark night's silence and humble reverence. Something is deposited deep within, and it is growing and active in me long before I become reflectively conscious of it. I do not create, achieve or produce it. I believe because I cannot *not* believe even as I cannot *not* be conscious that I am who I am and no one else. This intuition and sense of faith continues to grow and survive through all the seasons and turmoil of my life and consciousness. Who knows how one grows into that awareness of oneself which is utterly unshareable and incommunicable? I remember vividly seeing my father kneel by his bed each night with bowed head, being present to Someone whom I could not see but whom I felt through his prayer. I remember my mother getting up early each morning to go to the 6:30 Mass and sensed her carrying the whole family with her. I grew up in a Scottish-Irish neighborhood parish in the southwest side of Detroit which would have rivalled any medieval village in faith. By some spiritual process of osmosis, I was saturated by the prayer and faith of family and parish that opened a well in me, one which sinks deeper and deeper, and continues to baptize me with the ever-fresh water of life. I have come to know myself as an Irish peasant, possessed more by God than possessing him. He is with me. He walks before me. It is in my blood to pray and the breastplate of St. Patrick expresses my consciousness of Presence:

> I rise today through a mighty strength,
>   the invocation of the Trinity,
>   through a belief in the Threeness,
>   through confession of the Oneness
>   toward the Creator.
> Christ with me, Christ before me,
>   Christ behind me,
> Christ in me, Christ beneath me,
>   Christ above me
> Christ on my right, Christ on my left
>   Christ where I lie, Christ where I sit.
>   Christ where I arise,
> Christ in the heart of every man who thinks
>   of me
>   Christ in the mouth of every man who
>   speaks of me
>   Christ in every eye that sees me,
>   Christ in every ear that hears me.

My peasant faith has grown out of a community fire-tested for over fifteen hundred years. Each generation has saved itself but by a thread of God's mercy. What but his presence could have enabled us to continue to walk "into the endless desert of God's silence." How often like Elijah have I cried out, "I have had enough. Take my life" (I Kings 19:4); and like Jeremiah said, "I will not think about him, I will not speak in his name any more" (Jeremiah

20:9). Psalm 139 haunts me, "Where could I go to escape your spirit? Where could I flee from your presence?" With Jeremiah I confess, "You have seduced me, Lord, and I have let myself be seduced: you have overpowered me: you were the stronger" (Jer. 20:7). On my knees I pray with Job's tongue, "I am the man who obscured your designs with my empty-headed words. I have been holding forth on matters I cannot understand, on marvels beyond me and my knowledge. I knew you then only by hearsay; but now, having seen you with my own eyes, I retract all I have said, and in dust and ashes I repent" (Job 42,1).

The Father so loves the world, so loves us that he has sent the best of himself, all that he could give, his Son, to be with us forever. His love is always and everywhere at work, forgiving, recreating us, drawing us into himself. He is loving us at this moment with the love which he has for his own Son. "As the Father loves me so I have loved you." Prayer is responding, sensing this incomprehensible love which I am! His love is circumferential, 360°. I am so blind, so dumb, so crippled that I take in a few degrees only. I wait at my poor little window where once I caught a glimpse; but he is knocking at 359 other doors, windows, roofs, cellars and I am too stubborn to listen. For myself, to believe is to pray. Like Dag Hammarskjold I dare to say, "because I am, therefore he is." Everything is gift; therefore I thank him. I see his fingerprints, love prints, breath prints everywhere. What is there which is not a sacrament of his presence? Each one is loved by Father, Son and Holy Spirit, is "graced."

This experience of "grace," this gentle breath of his love, this indefinable "mysticism" of everyday is the center and source of prayer. He cannot love a little; he cannot love partially. He loves us this day with the fullness of love which will be ours for all eternity; it is our human overcast which prevents the enjoyment of the eternal sun of his love. Karl Rahner writes, "This mysticism is one of the normal and natural things in Christian experience which no one can avoid, even if he overlooks it, or cannot understand it, or sets it aside as something he does not want to think about." Prayer raises to consciousness this primal experience of being grasped by him, known by him. We are all too hesitant to believe deeply enough the mystery of the sacraments. At least on an elementary level, in the ordinary growth in faith of a Christian, the sacraments involve something mystical, something entailing immediate conscious contact with the person of Jesus. This conscious contact is seldom an overwhelming experience. It is barely perceptible. Yet one must be ready and waiting, looking for him. There must be a prophetic expectation. "So I say to you: Ask and it will be given to you; search and you will find; knock and the door will be opened to you.

For the one who asks always receives; the one who searches always finds; the one who knocks will always have the door opened to him. . .how much more will the heavenly Father give the Holy Spirit to those who ask him!" (Luke 11,9).

Let us never forget that Jesus is not a remote past. He is a presence and a power, alive, active as a two-edged sword. "Now I have opened in front of you a door that nobody will be able to close" (Rev. 3,8). "Look, I am standing at the door, knocking. If one of you hears me calling and opens the door, I will come in to share his meal, side by side with him" (Rev. 3,20). Only Jesus keeps his promises. "I have made you known to them and will continue to make you known so that the love with which you loved me may be in them and so that I may be in them" (John 17,26). These are the splendid, shining promises, true promises. But we can disregard them, refuse to believe. Then, as Sebastian Moore says, "The effect of being continually exposed to the truth which is doing one no good is distressing to the soul. There can even result a kind of unbelief, an exhaustion of the spirit which is all the worse for being partly conscious."

It is not enough to think about prayer, to read about it, to repeat the practices of one's childhood. Prayer is like swimming—one can learn only by doing it. It is like love and friendship, a work, a joy of one's whole lifetime. It is a marriage continually lost, continually found.

While there are many in our day who express a skepticism about prayer, many who have ceased to pray, nevertheless in the grace of God, in the movement of the Spirit, there has been a return to prayer. It has become popular, a movement. This prayer movement compels us to understand more radically and thoroughly the essence of Christian prayer. For all prayer is not Christian prayer. "It is not every spirit, my dear people, that you can trust; test them to see if they come from God; there are many false prophets now in the world" (John 4:1).

In Christian prayer there is only one priest, one mediator, one pray-er; Jesus Christ. The reality is Christ (Col: 2,17). There is only Christ: he is everything and he is in everything (Col: 3,11). There is only one name under heaven by which men can be saved. What makes prayer Christian is to know deeply Jesus in prayer and prayer in Jesus. When the Christian prays he knows that it is Jesus who prays within him, and that he is in Jesus. He experiences Jesus, knows and is known of him. The presence of Jesus in us is a compelling force and power. In Eucharist he renders us more and more present to one another and to ourselves. More and more he deposits in our lives his power to love, to render him present, to consecrate ourselves as he consecrated himself. The source and summit, the alpha and omega of Christian prayer is the Eucharist. There is no other prayer possible for the Christian whether he recognizes it or not. Vatican II has opened us to the Prayer of the Word which is inseparable from consecration and communion. Let us focus our attention on this Prayer of Communion which is the sacrament of prayer—Jesus in Prayer; and on the Prayer of Consecration which is the sacrament of ministry—Prayer in Jesus.

In Christian prayer Jesus confronts both the Christian and the non-Christian with radical decision. He leaves no room for a middle ground, for compromise. "I am the Way, the Truth, and the Life. No one can come to the Father except through me" (John 14:6). "I tell you emphatically, anyone who does not enter the sheepfold through the gate but gets in some other way is a thief and a seducer." "Enter by the narrow gate since the road that leads to perdition is wide and spacious and many take it; but it is the narrow gate and a hard road that leads to life and only a few find it" (Mt. 7:13). These are hard sayings, words which deeply disturb. There is an arrogance about them which often embarrasses the Christian. They are divisive, an obstacle, foolishness and madness to those who are not ready to understand. Jesus knew that this would be the result of his sayings: "Do you suppose that I am here to bring peace on earth? No, I tell you, but rather division" (Luke 2:51). "If anyone is ashamed of me and my words, the Son of Man will also be ashamed of him when he comes in the glory of his Father" (Mark 8:38).

Time does not dim the bluntness nor the strangeness of his words. Before Jesus broke into our history, became known to us, prayer was relatively simple. Few find difficulty with the prayer of nature, the prayer of interpersonal love, the prayer of cosmic quiet, of being at home in one's transcendental center. It is when the Son of God becomes man that all is changed, everything is sprung into an endless dawn of new life. "Now I am making the whole of creation new. . .I am the Alpha and the Omega, the Beginning and the End, Yesterday and Today, Now and Forever." "In bringing himself," says St. Irenaeus, "Christ has brought all newness." "If anyone is in Christ, he is a new creature." Christ brings us new wine, a new Spirit, a new Covenant in his Blood, in his Spirit. There is a new man, a new Adam. "The inner man in us is being renewed day by day" (Cor. 4:16).

In Christian prayer we are renewed through what can only be called a spiritual revolution, a putting on of "the new self that has been created in God's way, in the goodness and holiness of the truth" (Eph. 4:23). Our prayer is the celebration of being loved each day into new life, rejoicing with him who is born more fully in us. The Good News is not Christ's unless it is always good and ever *new*, now. Each day he sends his Spirit that our "hidden self" may grow strong. Each day is Bethany, Tabor, Emmaus. Above all, for a Christian in prayer, each day is Nazareth. The Annunciation is the crystal and prism of all Christian prayer. "Rejoice, Mary, the Lord loves you very dearly. He is with you. . .the Holy Spirit will come upon you." For us, "the Holy Spirit has poured into our hearts the love of God." The Spirit is with us in our weakness, "for when we cannot choose words to pray properly, the Spirit himself expresses our plea in a way that could never be put into words" (Romans 8:26). It is the Spirit Who hovers over the darkness of the depths of our inner being to bring forth the Christ within us (Ephesians 3).

When we can say with Paul, "It is no longer I who live, but Christ who lives within me;" when we can believe with our total being "There is only Jesus. He is everything; he is in everything;" when we understand, "Where he comes, there he is: and where he is, there he comes. . .and everything in which he is is in him, for he never goes out of himself (Ruysbroeck)—then we truly know Jesus in prayer, and know that our prayer is in Jesus. "Through him, with him, in him." "He Who eats my flesh and drinks my blood lives in me and I live in him" (John 6:56).

We know through our own experience that the kind of faith which Paul expresses never comes easily to man. If we could only believe the truth! "Lord, that I may see." "Help my unbelief." We know, in fact, that faith is impossible for man alone. "Without me you can do nothing." Yet Christ extravagantly pours the Gift into our hearts, filters it into our consciousness. We are haunted by the refrain, "There is One among you whom you do not recognize." Again and again at our Samaritan wells he softly speaks, "If you but knew the gift of God and who it is that is asking you for a drink!" The more one reads and prays the Gospel of John, the more the mind and heart swirl, as if in an electric blender, as again and again, over and under, up and down he repeats, "That all may be one as you, Father, are in me and I in you." That they may be one, as we are one, I living in them, you living in me." "Father, I want those you have given me to be with me where I am." Here is Jesus in prayer— to prayer in him are we called.

This is the ultimate God-shock—that we are *in Christ*, that he is in us. More than a hundred times in his letters Paul uses the expression, "In Christ." He is not speaking figuratively but declaring a mystical contact and identification with Christ. He writes from the depth of his own experience and the continued experience of the Christian community. There abounds a "third consciousness," that of being moved

by the Spirit of Jesus, his two-edged Word.
The Christian community lived in a vivid
growing consciousness of the closeness of
the Lord, in continual expectation of his
coming, of his gifts. Nor has the experience
of the first generation ceased. Down to our
own day every Christian generation cher-
ishes and rejoices in the words of Luke, "I
bless you, Father, Lord of heaven and earth
for hiding these things from the learned
and the clever and revealing them to mere
children. . .no one knows who the Son is
except the Father, and who the Father is
except the Son and those to whom the Son
chooses to reveal him." Then turning to his
disciples he spoke to them in private,
'Happy the eyes that see what you see for I
tell you that many prophets and kings
wanted to see what you see, and never saw
it; to hear what you hear, and never heard
it.' "

The joy of Jesus—"filled with joy by the
Holy Spirit"—the Christian joy will always
be a shock to human intelligence. Who can
grasp the mystery of the Incarnation continued in us? Who can fathom the mystery
that we are the Body of Christ with a
literalness we dare not utter. Rarely heard
today is the vocabulary of mystical theology: identification and union with Christ;
indwelling of the Trinity; deification
through participation. All of this is far
beyond us. Yet there are moments, hints,
intimations of the mystical in each of our
lives. Yeats called it, "The wind that

awakens the stars is now stirring in my blood." There is something, someone, at the edge of my consciousness beyond the realms of being. The Word of the Gospel brings into consciousness the reality already active in the depths of our person. "The Holy Spirit is given to us so that we may understand the gift we have already received." Again and again this capacity, this longing for God is activated in us. We are a harp of God waiting for his touch, a reed instrument ready for his breath. His is the Word which springs into our awareness, his the music which rises out of our heart.

God is not outside of us, apart from us, but within us. He is a presence, present to us. What makes us distinctively human is our capacity for conscious presence and relationship with each other. It is to the glory of man that he can become present to another; but this presence, to be complete, must stem from the presence of God. To enter into the presence of one another is a rich and deep experience, but it is a partial one. God is, however, *total presence* and relationship. He is *love*, always bringing us to his fullness of presence and relationship. Prayer is an entering into his love, into his presence, allowing him to enter our presence and love. The fullness of divinity indwells in Christ. In his humanity he was totally open to the Father. "I am never alone, the Father is always with me." Jesus enters into our presence and leads us into his presence and love of the Father! Thus, in our humanness we can be his presence in the world, we can become more and more his presence.

As we are drawn into his presence, we become more aware of Jesus at work in us. "The Father goes on working and so do I." His presence can never be simply static; it is dynamic, operative, interactional. He is always giving, communicating power to be more and more his—a new mind, a new heart, a new creature. We grow in awe of the gift of our own existence. Because Christ was human we come to love our own humanness. All is paradox. In our growing awareness of him we have increased awareness of ourselves. The more he pours into us the more we wish to pour ourselves out into him. He resembles us more than we resemble him. As he sinks his roots every more deeply into our being we want to pour ourselves out; yet, at the same time, we want to pour ourselves in, into him who dwells within us.

We carry with us always a sense of our own presence but we rarely reflect upon it; it is merely there. There are many facets, heights and depths in our own presence and in our presence to one another, but the deepest presence to ourselves is the presence which breaks into his presence. God's presence is always a gift, continually being given. He cannot be otherwise for he is love; he is Gift. If we desire it, sometimes even if we do not desire it, Jesus draws us

into the relationship of his never-ending life
and love with his Father. "Where I am I
want you to be." He imprints on our
consciousness the life which has already
begun in us, because he lives in us. He
continues to uncover to us who he is and
who he can come to be because of our
response to his dwelling in us. We are ever
changing, moving, struggling, alive in every
fiber, but at the same time ever related to
the life he lives within us, the life we bring
to him. Our growth in him, his growth in us
are correlative to the contrast between
them. "I am the Vine, you are the branches." "Without me you can do nothing." "I
will draw all men to myself." He is the
head of the whole body. No one is exempt
from *configuration with Christ*. He has
identified with all of us by taking our sins
upon himself; we are plunged into his death
that we may rise with him. Paul speaks
again and again of the meaning of Christ's
life, death and resurrection. "The secret is
this; Christ is in you." "All of you, then,
are Christ's body and each one is a part of
it." "We were baptized into Christ Jesus.
When we were baptized we went into the
tomb with him and joined him in death, so
that as Christ was raised from the dead by
the Father's glory, we too might live a new
life."

So all of us, in union with Christ, form
one body and as parts of it we belong to
one another. By Baptism and Eucahrist a
Christian is so closely united to Christ that

his life, suffering and death can be mystically attributed to Christ living in him and being glorified in him. God is love and each of us is an act of his love, we are his image, we are like him. We do not recognize what we are, what we are to become. There is a secret, a hidden self in us; it is himself. The ongoing act of creation by which we exist is his love which continues us in being. Incredible restraint on the part of God that his power, his love do not overwhelm our freedom! It is like harnessing atomic power to light a cigarette or dispatching a 747 to deliver a single piece of mail.

We have been given by God the radiant knowledge that we belong to him. We come from him, we return to him. Each day our life is given to us. Each of us, in ourselves, is a whole cosmos, a whole creation. Each man has greatness simply because he exists. It is easy to forget this because there are so many of us. The primitive with all his idols, because he saw God everywhere and in everything, was perhaps closer to God, much closer to his real self. Each of us is worth a book of poetry. As Thornton Wilder puts it, "Do any human beings ever realize life while they live it—every, every minute?. . .No, the saints and poets, maybe—they do some." Each of us is worthy of a little adoration. God "adores" man far more than man can adore God. God gives himself to man in a way man does not and cannot give himself to God. God loves man madly, foolishly, absurdly. God loves man

as man has never been able to love man.
The secret power and mystery of God at
work in man!

Jesus' love penetrates us, his presence
enables us to have greater presence and
consciousness, greater and greater love.
Simple presence leads into the presence of
love. How we are transformed by love!
How another's presence fills us; we are no
longer our own! How others draw us into
their presence, into their goodness unbe-
known to themselves! Their presence and
love activate, fill us, free us from ourselves,
free us for greatness. They energize us; we
absorb their love, their faith, their hope.
We absorb their life in a way we cannot
absorb the food and drink we take into our
body each day. Food and drink are spent
and dissipated within the same day. We
cannot eat for a week all at once, or sleep
for a week all at once. We cannot expand
or push too far beyond the demands of
eating and sleeping, the rhythm of working
and resting. But there is no limit to the
cumulative presence of love which sustains
the deeper life. God's kingdom grows as we
grow; we are his kingdom made visible,
bearing fruit. Whatever prayer we make, it
is Jesus praying in us, drawing us into
prayer in Jesus. He is teacher; he is
prompter.

In this prayer we are born again from
within. It is not the seed of death which we
carry within but the seed of life. Not
merely for nine months but for the whole

of our lives are we being born into eternal life. The inner life and light absorb more and more of the outer man as we allow him to transform us. "Give us this day our daily bread," we ask, and he responds, "This is my Body, take and eat; this is my Blood, take and drink." How little we understand. Our moments of insight are brief as the light of meteor in the night sky. But there are moments. Last summer I remember waiting for the sunrise near Rye Beach, New Hampshire. As I watched the first burst of the morning sun dance across the ocean toward me, the almost microscopic marine life at the water's edge drew me near. There was hardly a ripple on the surface. An utter silence entered me and I was more quiet than the ocean. The tide was beginning to come in and as I watched its gentle pattern, I suddenly became conscious that the ocean was breathing! The whole ocean was breathing in the rhythm of my own breath.

I have come to associate this experience of quiet with the moments of prayer after Eucharist, after receiving the Body and Blood of Christ. I am inwardly quiet, quiet as the depth of the ocean. Whose breath is that breathing in me? "I live, now not I, but Christ lives in me." The intimacy of communion is embarrassing. The intensity of feeling can be overwhelming. The intimate conversation with one whom you love leaves you open and vulnerable. These are the moments of unrecognized mystical experience in carnal knowledge, the divine become flesh in sacrament.

These are the moments of privileged prayer, of openness to the unique gift of prayer in Eucharist. Such experiences in our lives would seem to be those which we would most wish to hold, to have stay with us like the "stay with us" moment of Emmaus and "it is good for us to be here" of the Transfiguration. There is an after-glow to shared intimacy, we linger over the embers of the hearth, we savor the continued taste of an exquisite dinner. Strangely, though, we break off our communion prayer as if we were either afraid or unable to sustain it. The experience of that kind of love so frightens us in its burning intensity that we intuitively insulate ourselves, put up our shield.

Yet Christ continues to give himself to us. We scarcely dare to believe that he experiences joy in his giving, in his communion with us. "Like a mother's joy when her baby is smiling into her eyes for the first time," wrote Dostoevsky, "so is God's joy when one of his children turns and prays to him for the first time."

When we turn out hearts to Christ and *ask,* he answers. The cumulative dynamic presence of him in resurrection in us raises our whole consciousness. We take him to ourselves, he takes us to himself. It is an ongoing kind of transubstantiation as he comes into us, and our life passes over into his life. We carry his life within us for the whole of our lives. He makes us into Eucharist, incorporating us more and more into himself.

We grow into the body of Christ like the vine grows into the earth. A mother carries life within her for nine months; we carry his life within us the whole of our lives and he makes us into Eucharist, incorporating us more and more into himself. The changing of bread and wine is but the beginning, the promise of what he does in us. We are continually growing into the fullness of Christ's humanity and divinity. Because the interflow and infusion of his Spirit never wanes, there is increasingly more of him in us. A new psychological life begins in us. The mystical sacramental presence of Christ in us gives us a conscious permanent contact with the Father, gives us an illumination of our understanding of him "who has made his light shine in our hearts" (2 Cor. 3,18).

As our lives become more open to him, we have a heightened awareness that each day he shepherds, draws and guides us. We are aware that we never quite complete our thanksgiving, that we are compelled to return to him again and again in a deep sense of gratitude. Through the layers of our unconscious, he penetrates, awakens us to faith-consciousness. His love calls us to abandon what we know for what we will not know until we rest in the Divine indwelling.

The Divine Indwelling is a compelling, overwhelming truth. The beautiful Latin word is *circuminsessio*, meaning, "sitting around inside of each other." It is the penetration and indwelling of the three divine persons reciprocally in one another and in us. In our family life we come to experience the inflowing of another's presence, our father's or mother's, brother's or sister's. The penetration and saturation is so total that one even begins to look like the other so that the other is no longer other but one's self.

As we understand more deeply this Divine Indwelling, we know also that Love is not love until it is given away. God is not God until he is given away. Only in the mystery of the Incarnation, only in his continued guarantee, sign and seal in the Eucharist, do we begin to glimpse the grandeur of the Father's *kenosis*, the emptying of himself in order to fill us with his Son. We shall never wholly comprehend the gift of Jesus in us, to us.

In the gift is the promise, "Whoever believes in me will perform the same works as I do myself; he will perform even greater works." Jesus' indwelling in us is not static. This presence in us has consequences. Jesus expects much from us. "I commission you to go out and bear fruit, fruit that will last" (John 15,16). And Paul continues, "so that the saints together make a unity, building up the Body of Christ. In this way we all are to come to unity in our faith and in our knowledge of the Son of God, until we become the perfect Man, fully mature with the fullness of Christ himself. Then we shall not be children any longer." "If we live by the truth and in love, we shall grow in all ways into Christ, who is the Head, by whom the whole body is fitted and joined together, every joint adding its own strength, for each separate part to work according to its function. So the body grows until it has built itself up in love" (Eph. 4,13).

These sayings speak of the ongoing process of our transformation into Jesus who fills us with his presence, his love, his word. The transformation takes place in the quiet, as we wait for him and pray in the words we have. "Behold I stand at the door and knock; if any man open, I will come in." "In quiet and confidence shall be your strength." Instead of hammering at the gates of heaven, we are told to open our hearts, to wait and pray. Jesus responds not so much to our impatient demand for a sign; but to our waiting patiently for him, our becoming conscious that he has all the time been there, in us.

When Jesus prays in us, it is in creative and redemptive love, imparting to us his Spirit, that we can love as he loves, can love him with his own love, loving as the Father loved him. In communion, he renders us more and more present to ourselves, depositing in our lives his power to love, to render present, to consecrate, to pray.

The ultimate act of Christ's prayer was to lay down his life for us. "He had always loved those who were his in the world; now he showed how perfect his love was (John 13,1). The prayer of the Eucharistic communion is the sacrament of prayer. Because he has shown us the depth of prayer, we can respond only in love, in humility, in abandonment to him. This is prayer.

Once and forever in this abandonment of Christ, he consecrated himself. His act of consecration, of love, gave everything to everyone forever. We are able to make our act of consecration one day at a time with what we have to bring to it at the moment. His commandment, "Do this in memory of me" continues its imperative.

If we respond to this imperative, his incarnational reality accumulates in us. He calls us, deepens our capacity to love, to be consecrated, to pray, to die and to rise. Our growth deepens in us, also, in a new awareness, in a new humility.

Humility and reverence before one another and before God create in us a gradual and profound effect. "Everything that happens," says Rilke, "keeps on being a beginning." This truth is reflected in the Eucharist. Each consecration makes us new persons—the "new" in us discovering the "new" in others. We become transparent and vulnerable. "For them I consecrate myself," Jesus said. And we, we make ourselves him that we may *be* for others. His hidden presence uncovers our hidden selves, opens to us the hidden presence of others. And the world becomes filled with the transparencies of God.

"It is only because God is with us that we can find him." "No one has ever seen God; it is the only Son who is nearest the Father's heart who has made him known." "No one can come to the Father except through me." Adoration and prayer are gifts. God is apprehended only if there be response on our part, seeking and response. It demands time and patience, patience with ourselves, a waiting for God. When we hear his call, "Come and see," and enter his presence day after day, our prayer makes us like delicate photosensitive plates to God, collecting his light. Finally we see in the darkness; and are able to cry out with Paul, in adoration, "I *know* in Whom I have believed."

(From *Surprised By The Spirit*, pp 31-2).

II. HOLY HOUR

A Co-worker must be able to give Jesus to the people. For that, we must be close to Jesus. We should have a Holy Hour for prayer and meditation. Even if there are only a few of us, we could have it in our local parish, wherever we are. If we are really to love the poor, then our first contact must be with him in the Blessed Sacrament. It is easy then to transfer the love we have for Jesus to the poor.

—Mother Teresa, October, 1972.

In October, when I was flying from Utah to Chicago with Mother Teresa, I asked her what she would do were she to give a retreat. I was hoping that she would outline an ideal retreat for me to use. She answered me typically in four words, "Let Jesus do it." I was left speechless; all my other questions faded. "Let Jesus do it." I eventually got her to elaborate further. "We have to be brought face to face with Jesus, not merely with the priest. Let there be exposition, Scripture, silence," were her suggestions. "The understanding which comes in prayer leads to love and love leads to service." What a beautiful theology of the Holy Hour!

The expression "Holy Hour" is an old term for a once popular devotion. But it will continue to be discovered anew because it is a Gospel event, an invitation coming directly from Christ himself at his great moment of suffering at Gethsemane. "Don't you have the strength to keep awake with me one hour?" (Matthew 26,41). I think of this as one of the great mysteries of the Gospel, that Jesus asked his disciples to be with him in his prayer. He needed them to be with him. He came back repeatedly to ask them to stay awake with him. What sadness must have filled him when he returned to see them asleep! What anguish in his words when he had to say, "You can sleep on now and take your rest. It is all over. The hour has come! (Mark 14,41).

The hour, in Greek kairos, is the hour when the Holy Spirit works; the moment when the Lord comes. To wake with Christ is to be ready when he comes, to watch with him. How beautiful the ancient tradition, ever new, of remaining awake for an hour to consecrate the night.

"Stay with me. Be with me" is the call of love, heart speaking to heart. Those whom he chooses he draws to himself. Where else is there to go? Lovers are forever drawn to the place where they last saw the beloved. It is by an intuition of the heart that we are drawn to the Eucharist to linger in his presence. The tabernacle is the guarantee that he has "pitched his tent" among us forever. (Tabernacle is the Latin word for tent). The tabernacle is a mirror of his presence within us; we are his temple more than any cathedral or basilica.

The Blessed Sacrament is the Mass held in meditation. The Eucharist is the sacrament of prayer, the source and summit of the Christian life. The Eucharistic reservation is the promise visibly kept that "He is living forever to intercede for all who come to God through him" (Hebrews 7,25). "There at God's right hand he stands and pleads for us" (Romans 8,35).

Like the Emmaus disciples we press him to stay with us and "do not our hearts burn within us as he talks to us and explains the scriptures to us" (Luke 24,32).

His Presence before us activates all his deposited and cumulative presence within us. His Presence stirs up the Spirit within us, fans the gray embers of our heart into deep communion. Karl Rahner does not hesitate to say that this kind of spiritual communion is sacramental, an action on his part, not merely a desire on our part!

The Holy Hour before the tabernacle cannot end there as did the Holy Hour of the past. That would be only part of the Eucharist. Our Lord gave the command, "Come," but he also commanded us to "Go." "If you love me, feed my sheep." The Holy Hour before the Eucharist is to lead to the Holy Hour with the poor, with those who enjoy little of human fulfillment, those whose only consolation is Jesus.

The Eucharist is the sacrament of the poor, the sacrament which leads, compels us to be identified with the poor because he was poor. Our Eucharist is incomplete if it does not lead us to the service and love of the poor. Our Holy Hour with him must draw us to our Holy Hour with his poor.

We deprive ourselves of a unique grace when we do not have direct contact with the poor. As Mother Teresa says often, "Christ comes to us under two forms, that of bread and that of the poor." The poor have a Eucharist to give to us. In receiving communion from them, we discover our own poorness. The poorer we are the more we recognize that everything is gift. Seeing everything and everyone as personal gift to us, we are continually drawn into thanksgiving, into a Eucharistic way of life which breathes joy, peace, hope.

There is never enough time in the action of the Mass for our thanksgiving. There is never enough time to recognize, to celebrate his love. So we are drawn to his sacramental presence again and again to linger awhile with him, to deepen our remembrance, to expand our anticipation of him. He comes to us in order to send us out to his little ones, to those who will come to know him only through us who are becoming his Eucharist.

The Holy Hour opens to us the depths of the Eucharist as the sacrament of prayer, the sacrament of the poor. "He emptied himself to become the poorest of the poor" (Phil 2,7). The Holy Hour before Jesus compels us to the holy hour with the poor.

VII DISCIPLE: WELCOMING THE RESURRECTION

"Why are you so surprised. . .it is really I" (Luke 24,38).

"I was dead and behold I am alive forever more" (Rev. 1,18).

"And there, coming to meet them, was Jesus" (Matthew 28,9).

On the third day he arose from death—Easter, Resurrection—what overwhelming thoughts! When we were children we celebrated this day with Easter baskets filled with chocolate eggs and candy bunnies. What a marvelous way for Easter joy to overflow and be experienced by his little ones. Perhaps as children we invited more of the Easter mystery than we can understand as adults. Year after year the cycle of Easter passes over us (Passovers us). Or perhaps it is we who pass through it. In the process something filters through to us, something is deposited in us. The Word of God pierces to the marrow of the soul. It slips into our perception and if it cannot command us it nevertheless haunts us with its subtle ways of nudging, drawing, grasping.

"And whoever lives and believes in me will never die."

"Do you believe this?" (John 11,26).

"Unless a wheat grain falls on the ground and dies, it remains only a single grain; but if it dies, it yields a rich harvest" (John 12,24).

What was the resurrection like for Jesus? This is a healthy question, one which springs from the curiosity of living faith. Ordinarily Scripture is very reserved in its expression of the great mysteries, and theology is limited by the reticence of Scripture. The Word of God beckons us to stretch our imaginations and hearts. "Since you have been brought back to true life with Christ, *you must look for the things that are in heaven,* where Christ is, sitting at God's right hand. *Let your thoughts be on heavenly things,* not on the things that are on the earth, because you have died, and now the life you have is hidden with Christ in God" (Col. 3,1).

The human fascination with the resurrection does not diminish for it is the central reality of our Faith, the fulfillment of man's greatest hope and dream. Every man desires to believe in the resurrection; at the same time he is held back by a most anguishing kind of fear: "What if it is not real?" The non-believer cries out, "If only it were true!" The believer with no less difficulty cries out, "If only I could believe the truth; help my unbelief!" "And on the third day he will rise again." "But they could make nothing of this; what he said was quite obscure to them, they had no idea what it meant" (Luke 18,34). Each of the Synoptics painfully emphasize the three distinct predictions and prophecies which Jesus made of his death and resurrection. The refrain is the same, "They did not understand." So much was "un-understood." Mark in his usual fashion describes vividly the disciples' lack of understanding: "They were on the road, going up to Jerusalem; *Jesus was walking on ahead of them;* they were in a daze, and those who followed were apprehensive" (Mark 10,32). Even on that *first day* of the week when Mary of Magdala, Peter and John experienced the empty tomb, John has to write, "Til this moment they had failed to understand the teaching of scripture, that he must rise from the dead" (John 20,10). Mark is more blunt about the disciples' reaction to the first witnesses of the Risen Jesus. "But they *did not believe* her (Mary of Magdala) when they heard her say that he was alive and that she had seen him" (Mark 16,11). Again with the Emmaus travelers, "These went back and told the others, who *did not believe* them either" (Mark 16,13). And finally Mark writes, when Jesus showed himself to the eleven while they were at table, "He reproached them for their incredulity and obstinacy, because *they had refused to believe* those who had seen him after he had risen"

(Mark 16,14). Luke is more gentle as he describes that Easter evening when he stood in their midst and asked them, "Why are you so surprised? And why are these doubts rising in your hearts? Look at my hands and feet; yes, *it is I.* Touch me and see for yourselves; a ghost has no flesh and bones as you can see I have. And as he said this he showed them his hands and feet." Then Luke continues, "Their joy was so great they could not believe it and they stood there dumbfounded." "So he said to them, 'Have you anything here to eat?' and they offered him a piece of grilled fish, which he took and ate before their eyes" (Luke 24,37).

John narrates the second appearance of Jesus to the disciples, emphasizing his sensitive concern for Thomas. What must have been Thomas' experience as the Lord spoke to him, commanded him, "Put your finger here; look, here are my hands. Give me your hand; put it into my side. Doubt no longer but believe." Thomas replied, "My Lord and my God." Jesus said to him:

"You believe because you can see me. Happy are those who have not seen and yet believe" (John 20,27).

We have not seen, yet there is nothing within us that demands, "Unless I see the holes that the nails made in his hands and can put my hand into his side, I refuse to believe" (John 20,25). We believe and have no need to weep, "They have taken my

Lord away and I don't know where they
have put him" (John 20,13). We envy the
women coming away from the tomb:
"There, coming to meet them, was Jesus"
(Matthew 28,9). What a moment! And here
again when we would most like a few
words of detail, the scripture is reticent,
wrapping, insulating her mystery in a grand
silence. Yet what could we say? What
dumb questions would be on our lips?
What could we understand more than that
understanding already given to us. Nevertheless, I am sure, even after all these years
of celebrating, meditating his resurrection
our human curiosity has endless questions
ready for our "third day." For what is of
greater "human interest" to us than his
resurrection. I wonder often what it was
like, that first conscious moment of Jesus
in the resurrection. What did he experience
in his human consciousness? What were his
thoughts and feelings as he rolled up "the
cloth that had been over his head (this was
not with the linen cloths but rolled up in a
place by itself" (John 20,7). The experience of human consciousness from Adam
to Christ—how much history is involved! I
have never been able to forget the creation
of Adam sequence in the movie, *The Ten
Commandments.* In the golden dawn man
stood upright, *opened* his eyes, looked
around at all of creation and *knew* what he
beheld—an indescribable and beautiful
moment, one in which each of us has
shared. But who among us can remember

those first conscious processes, so illusive were they. Who among us can know the unhindered fullness of Chirst's consciousness in the resurrection until such time as we enter into his eternal consciousness.

All the great moments of history, of human achievement pale before the moment of Christ's resurrection: the discovery of fire, tools, agriculture, the development of language, art, literature, the invention of the engine, airplane, rockets, atomic energy, walking on the moon.

All of history and eternity are changed in that first moment of the human consciousness of the Risen Christ. He had overcome the world, nature and death as well as sin—the great flaw in human freedom! For us everything depended upon that moment, all was suspended, waiting. "If Christ has not been raised then our preaching is useless and your believing, it is useless" (I Cor. 15,15). What must have been the joy in the human heart of Jesus! What must have been the peace-smile upon his face, the immense joy and peace in the unfolding of all that he had tried to say and do: redemption and resurrection of the whole world—man's freedom unbent—heaven opened—sin and death overcome—hopes and dreams of all the centuries realized—all men freed from their inability to love—the unity of mankind inaugurated.

Did there exist a thought in the mind and heart of Jesus? "Father, I did not think it would be so hard. You really meant it."

More probably all was forgotten, as creation standing on its tiptoes began to experience the new Spirit of life breathed and poured forth over all mankind. One can imagine the pleroma, the fullness of Jesus as he experienced the inexpressible gratitude of all men for all time slowly growing to an awareness, a conviction of resurrection with Christ.

His Spirit is being released over all of mankind, all of his life; truth, joy, peace is being poured into us. All that is human is eternalized; all that is divine is now ours in him. He is to be with us always, giving us a taste of what he is now, what we will become. He is drawing us into himself. Now he is ever present; he will not leave us friendless. Before the resurrection he was limited by bodily space to one house, one street, one city, one person, one group of people at a time. No longer is he confined to a limited circle of human presence. He comes fully to all those who desire and love him. ". . .And I shall love him and show myself to him. . .and my Father will love him, and we shall come to him and make our home with him" (John 14,21). From the resurrection on, Bloom remarks, "the heart of man opens into the depths of God."

The more I attempt to meditate on the resurrection the more I realize that Jesus has said all that could be said in the words of the Last Supper as narrated by John.

There is nothing more to say. "Of his fullness *(pleroma,* Spirit) we have all received." We are witnesses to the resurrection no less than the apostles and Paul, for the Risen Christ can be known only in faith. No one recognized what appeared before their senses. The only Jesus we can believe in is the risen Lord who draws us to himself, giving us his Spirit, enabling us to believe. If we believe, it is through his Spirit. The Spirit in us enables us to see the "glory" of the resurrection, not the *"kabod"* of the Old Testament, the dazzling display of power and might, but the quiet hidden glory of his annunciation, birth, Nazareth, Calvary now continued in water, bread and wine, oils, human words and hands, the sacraments of every day which transform us into a sacrament of Jesus. This is the glory, the joy, peace and communion that the world cannot perceive (I Cor. 2,12).

The resurrection continues to happen in us in our everydayness: "The water that I shall give will turn into a spring inside him, welling up to eternal life" (John 4,14). "I am the living bread which has come down from heaven. Anyone who eats this bread will live forever" (John 6,51). "I am the resurrection and the life. . .whoever lives and believes in me will never die" (John 11,26). What a staggering assertion: to live forever, never to die. It is a truth difficult to believe as Our Lord knows well. He immediately asks, "Do you believe this?"

(John 11,26). We say, "Yes," knowing how little we understand. We know we touch the miracle of Easter Life in Baptism pondering what can happen in an instant. The quantum leap from nothingness to life in the moment of conception, the moment of birth, of consciousness, of faith, of love; such is the mystery of baptism-resurrection now and at the hour of our death.

Easter life! One moment of life would have been enough—one moment of love, of consciousness, of truth, of joy. But we are called to live all these moments without end. Time shall be no more, "there will be no more death, and no more mourning or sadness. The world of the past has gone. . .Now I am making the whole of creation new. . .It is already done" (Rev. 21,4). His resurrection has begun the parousia, the world to come is here, the kingdom is in our midst.

All of earth resonates with the Spring abundance of life erupting lavishly. He gardens us, farms us. We are his fields which he waters, yielding thirty, sixty, a hundred-fold fruitfulness. "Scattering a thousand graces he passed through these groves in haste and looking upon them as he went left them by his glance alone clothed with beauty" (John of the Cross). "He saves what he is." Jesus alone can make all things endure. Everything of ours changes, fades, ages, diminishes. How fragile, how limited is our life! But now, "there, coming to meet us, is Jesus." This is the resurrection: Jesus coming to meet us, discovering us when we least expect him.

> "I hear my Beloved
> See how he comes
> Leaping on the mountains
> Bounding over the hills
> My Beloved is like a gazelle
> Like a young stag" (Song of Songs 2,8).

Jesus, so filled with life, now sustains each of our lives, drawing us into his life. Nothing will be lost! He has released all the energy, life, power of his Spirit into us. "The love of God has been poured into our hearts by the Holy Spirit which has been *given* us" (Romans 5,5). The resurrection is more than the faith event which began the Christian community 2000 years ago, it is our faith experience now unfolding through the deepening reality of Christ pouring his resurrection into us through his word and sacrament. The only Jesus we can touch is the Risen Jesus who dwells now with us. If he is not now with us, he will never be with us; our faith is foolish. If he is not contemporary, then he is not eternal. The life which he gives is his risen life. As the "last Adam," Jesus in his resurrection has become the "life-giving Spirit" (I Cor. 15,46), in whose image all mankind must be formed. This work of resurrection in time is an ongoing transformation already in progress in this life. "And we, with our unveiled faces reflecting like mirrors the brightness of the Lord, all grow brighter and brighter as we are turned into the image that we reflect; this is the work of the Lord who is Spirit" (II Cor. 3,18).

The resurrection is process and evolution. "The Father goes on *working* and so do I" (John 5,18). "All life, all holiness comes from you through your Son, Jesus Christ our Lord, by the *working* of the Holy Spirit" (III Eucharistic Prayer). Each year the resurrection reaches a new level, a new breadth, a new depth in the sacrament of the church, in the world. His life is rising, cresting in us ever more totally. Every moment of the resurrection has an eternal inexhaustive dimension. T. S. Eliot suggests that "Time future and time past are both perhaps present in time present." Time is nothing new under the sun except in the resurrection. This makes everything new! "Christ has brought all newness in bringing himself" (Irenaeus).

Even the modern sciences have opened us anew to the mystery of resurrection. Modern physics, the most materialistic of the sciences, has shown that when one reaches the atomic level, the objective world ceases to exist. The universe begins to look more like a great thought than a great machine. The affinity between fire and rose becomes more visible. Thus the resurrection can be recognized as more "real" than the physical, the material; more present, more effective.

There is a cosmic disclosure, something of his glory breaking through in the little moments of resurrection in us. The Lord keeps his promise to return, to dwell in us, to reveal himself to those who love him. He calls us out of the tomb of everydayness into daily newness of life. In our daily Bread the Risen Jesus invites a fresh response, a new thanksgiving which eternalizes, "forevers" each day. Nothing is really over! Something each day is permanently built, deposited in our bodies, minds, hearts, spirits. He allows us to experience the reality of his presence in history although he remains unseen. Much of our world lies in the darkness of the day of his death—God is dead; life is absurd. Many world religions are in the "second day" waiting for God to come. The Christian lives in the dawning light of the "third day." "He is not in the tomb, for he has risen as he said he would. . .then go quickly and tell his disciples, 'He has risen from the dead and now he is going before you to Galilee; it is there that you will see him'" (Matthew. 28,6).

Every Christian carries the "third day" within himself. New life is given to us. We are paschal candles, a light to the world, sent out to feed a world which hungers for the bread of the Word and Life. He goes before us into the Galilee of everydayness. He returns each day at Eucharist lest we forget, lest we fall victim to amnesia. The difficulty we experience in remembering to stay "in touch," to be present to that Someone, makes it imperative that we receive and continue to receive the Spirit of Jesus, the breath of his life, giving us each day his *new life*; changing our heart into his heart, our blood into his blood, our body into his body! So deep is the interpenetration between what he is doing and what I am doing that my prayer becomes his action; his prayer becomes my action.

We gather each day to meet him, to await him who will be human as we are for all eternity. What he is, I am becoming; where he is, he is praying I will be, drawing me there. The Good News is the resurrection. It will always be good, always be new. What can compare, be worthier of celebration than the realization that we are daily fed by the mystery of his resurrection, continually raised, lifted up by the Spirit of the Risen Christ who pours himself into us. Daily, in the Consecration of the Mass, we are changed by his life and his truth, more present, more powerful than before his death.

In the beautiful words of Caryll Houselander, "We are the resurrection, going on always, always giving back Christ's life to the world. . .We are to live the resurrection. It is to be a life of love, love that creates, that gives beauty to life. . .and he gives us his own power of consummated love to use for one another, to raise one another from the dead. The ultimate miracle of Divine Love is this, that the life of the Risen Christ is given to us to give to one another, through the daily bread of our human love" *(The Risen Christ)*.

VIII LETTER FROM SACRED HEART SEMINARY

I did not know where I would be writing my letter this year. So many places would have lent themselves: Brownsville, Texas, Diocesan Priests' Retreat. Orange, California, St. Joseph Sisters. Denver, Colorado, Sisters of Charity. Rye Beach, New Hampshire, Christian Brothers. Hampton Bays with the Dominican Sisters of the Sick Poor. Memphis, Tennessee with the Poor Clares. Nauvoo, Illinois with the Benedictines. Burlingame, California with the Mercy Sisters. Melbourne, Florida with the Adrian Dominicans. Dubuque, Iowa with the Franciscans. Dublin, Carrick-on Shannon, Ireland with the relatives. Oxford, England at the Cistercians—Orthodox Symposium. Portland, Oregon, four parishes. Spokane, Washington, Franciscan Sisters of Perpetual Adoration. Harlem, Mother Theresa of Calcutta. New Melleray, Iowa, Trappists. Honolulu, Sisters of St. Joseph Corondolet.

With almost six months of the year spent on the road, in the air, I am beginning to feel like an itinerant preacher. As time goes on I have come to appreciate the deep joy of coming home to my city, to Sacred Heart Seminary. Airports have become my "wayside chapels." The excitement of moving down the runway and rising into the stratosphere is as intense as my first experience of it. I am filled with the same awe when I view the entire metropolitan area unfolded below the wing tip, God's eye view of my city. And something within draws me to utter a blessing over the city, nothing dramatic, just a one-finger sign of the cross. I feel the same delight when we break through the overcast into the blue sky and full shining sun, the sign of his faithful love. And I am reminded that he who is faithful cannot love us more or less; he must love totally, completely. He loves us at this moment as fully as he will love us forever. Only our human overcast prevents our recognizing, our experiencing this inexhaustible, extravagant love.

As we glide over the city I am reminded, too, of my chalice. The base is transparent rock crystal, supporting the large gold-hammered cup. Around the outside of the cup in cloisonne enamel is the skyline of Detroit. Above it is the crucifix with four drops of blood falling upon the city, an interpretation of John of the Cross' vision of Christ hanging upon the cross until the end of time in his suffering Body, the Church.

On my returns to Detroit I experience a gradual awakening in myself of the presence of all those persons I have known, all those I carry within me. I feel welcomed by the cumulative deposit of my life and presence in them. Again I bless the city with a blessing of thanksgiving and joy for a fruitful trip, a safe return. Opening at random my pocket Scripture, as is my custom when landing or departing, I find a thought which very often is prophetic of the day.

Sacred Heart Seminary College is located in the heart of the City, a mile west of the Cathedral, a mile and a half on a northwest diagonal from the General Motors Building, the International Headquarters of G. M. It is centered in the Police Tenth Precinct, which has a reputation for the highest crime and murder rate in the entire world. The seminary's two hundred foot Gothic tower is the landmark of the neighborhood.

The main door of the college leads one beneath the tower and into the large chapel. On a sunny afternoon the eye is immediately captivated by the great stain glass window of Christ the Good Shepherd over the altar and reredos with its wooden carvings of the Twelve Apostles. The chapel is spacious and majestic, yet at the same time austere in its simplicity. It is here in this place that I have prayed for over half of my life—eight years as a student, thirteen years as a member of the faculty. It is a holy place, a place of great prayer, of great wrestling. One is immediately enveloped in the cumulative prayer of the thousand priests who have lived and prayed here. The cornerstone, carrying the inscription in Latin, "I will give you shepherds with my own heart," reminds one of the countless mysteries of grace unfolded here! "God writes straight in crooked lines."

I remember a remark I made once to Bill Downey when we were college sophomores. Bill said what he would most like to do as a priest would be to teach in the seminary. My instantaneous response was, "That is the last thing in the world I would want to do." How well, how strangely we utter prophecies over our own lives, even though negatively at times. I put the conversation out of my mind until ten years later when I was asked to teach at the seminary—and of all possible subjects, Latin and Greek. Everything within me cried, "No." This was the only thing I had excluded from my priestly ministry—Seminary work. God alone knew it; only he could ask it. There was nothing I cared less to do and I raged violently within myself that I would not, could not do it. Yet all the while I knew that he left me no other choice; I could not do otherwise.

I went to my Spiritual Director at the seminary, Father Lynch, and told him of my predicament. He just laughed and told me to pray about it. I took a week of my vacation and went to the Trappist Monastery of Genesee near Rochester, New York. In my three years of parish work at St. Peter's in Harper Woods I had often longed for more time to pray. Now I had eight full days and the holy Trappist Monks to support me. My first opportunity I went to the Abbot and asked him to teach me to pray. He did not live up to my expectations which is probably more a commentary on myself. I had hoped that he would teach me three easy steps to contemplation and also lead me there in eight days. Never had I experienced more time to pray, never did I feel the poverty of my prayer more deeply.

With reluctant abandonment I began my year of graduate work in Latin and Greek. Then followed six years of teaching. This is now my seventh year as Spiritual Director in the very room where I first protested that I could not do it.

My room is on the second floor, the first room east of the Gothic Tower. My desk is located before three eight-by-two arched windows facing out on the Boulevard and the four-storied apartment buildings across the way. The window sill is laced with artifacts which echo my favorite people and places from around the world. Centered in the middle window is a relic of the true cross companioned by a vigil light of glass mosaic from Sausalito, several prehistoric fossils, coral from Hawaii, geode from Mexico, ceramic pieces from my students, etc. In the east corner of the room near the window is an antique hand-carved prie-dieu which belonged to my first and only pastor, Father Michael Collins. I seldom use it for praying but occasionally I like to kneel upon it in the darkness and look out over my city. How much hidden life before me in the four-storied apartments across the boulevard with the crossword-puzzle lights, the intermittent headlights of the late night traffic, the slow revolving "Shell" sign at the corner gas station. Rare the hour when police siren, fire truck or ambulance warning does not pierce the night. Each siren is a call for help, for prayer. "Lord go to their assistance, make haste, hurry to help them."

As I kneel in thought/prayer at my window looking across at the apartments, I often wonder if anyone there kneels at his window looking unknowingly my way. I think often of those who drive by my window each day, driving through my/our "prayer field" unawares. I like to think of the seminary as a prayer field similar to a magnetic field or field of force with an unknown "range" of prayer and love. Students frequently abbreviate the seminary name referring to it simply as "the Heart." I think this is an excellent description of the work of the seminary community—the radiation of the prayer and love embedded in the hearts of these young men. The lifestream of a diocese is its seminary. The hope and promise of the future Church is in the faith, the boldness of these young men. In these turbulent times when so many experience the flickering flames of a dying vocation, what greater evidence for the action and inspiration of the Holy Spirit than these young men aspiring to follow Christ totally. Finding deep support in Paul's words, *"Here we are, fools* for the sake of Christ" (I Cor 4,10), they dare to "love God madly, knowing there is so little time." The foolishness of the priesthood!

In the Eastern Church "Fool for Christ's Sake" is a category of saint as is "Martyr" or "Virgin" and has its own proper liturgical material. If Christ, the Master, was accused of madness, so can the disciple expect like treatment. Intuitively he knows that "it is the highest wisdom to be thought mad for the love of Christ." "Their eyes blaze fire, but their shoulders sag as if under a great weight."

To be a fool for Christ is difficult, for understanding is a basic need of the human person. To be a fool for Christ goes beyond the misunderstanding of a conversation, of an action, of a project, to strike at the core and direction of one's whole life. It is to be alienated, dropped from one's society and culture. It is to become a marginal man, doubting one's reason, one's heart, one's sanity. It is to become a displaced person in contemporary life. It is to find oneself where Jesus is most at home.

Temptations come: how difficult to give one's self to prayer and study when you desire with all your heart to lay down your life for others. How difficult to accept the hidden life of Nazareth when the rest of the world appears to be in revolution. But also comes the ever deepening realization that one is called to be the man of prayer,

the man of deep faith, and he makes his
own the words of Karl Rahner:

> The priest is not an angel sent from heaven.
> He is a man chosen from among members of
> the church, a Christian. Remaining man and
> Christian, he begins to speak to you the
> word of God.
>
> This word is not his own. No, he comes to
> you because God has told him to proclaim
> God's word.
>
> Perhaps he has not entirely understood it
> himself. Perhaps he adulterates it. But he
> believes, and despite his fears he knows that
> he must communicate God's word to you.
>
> For must not some one of us say something
> about God, about eternal life, about the
> majesty of grace in our sanctified being;
> must not some one of us speak of sin, the
> judgment and mercy of God?
>
> So my dear friends, pray for him. Carry him
> so that he might be able to sustain others by
> bringing to them the mystery of God's love
> revealed in Christ Jesus.

A student theologian from another seminary once wrote to me about his desire to
pray and his search for God. He asked:
"How does one pray when he cannot go to
the desert or to an island? How does one
pray, love in the vast industrial city where
there seems to be more evil than good?"
My experiences at Assekrem in the Sahara

and on Cat Island are indelible and continue with me. Yet when I reflect back upon these times in my life, I look upon them not so much as summit experiences but as times when there took place within me a great gathering and drawing together of all that had gone before. I went seeking, only to discover the gifts which I had already received.

When I first returned from Assekrem, I received this letter from a friend:

Father Farrell:

Along the way, as I was reading your letter, I was, frankly, overtaken by the emotion of jealousy and envy. And, I said to myself, "why should he have this great experience? Why does he merit these great soul resting experiences, these refresheners of the spirit and these rare opportunities of communicating with God?

Then as I was reading I suddenly became conscious of my own desert experience. The difference between our experiences is that I am still in the desert and you are home. How I got into the desert I can't truthfully recall. I do recall being in a rather green pasture very well nourished by nature, and in no way arid. Suddenly, however, I realized I was in the desert and it was lonely, dry and frighteningly insecure. At the time I arrived I was certain God was with me. But then, apparently out of distraction, I discovered he had disappeared. And from my desert hermitage I shouted out to him but got no response. . .not even an acho from across the mountain. Then I panicked! Had I lost him, or had he lost me? And, what do I do now? Which way to go in search for him? Or should I remain in my hermitage and hope he will find me?

At this writing the sun comes up blazingly hot, but the night is devoid of the stars, the moon and the glory of the night. And I wonder where he is and what he is doing. Does he know I am looking for him, or has he come upon other friends and is secure in some oasis.

Shortly I'll need to make a decision for I cannot go on much longer in this hermitage. The food is good, there is adequate water and the tent is comfortable. But the desert is lonely and I long for friendship. And I worry that I may have estranged myself from him.

Maybe we'll meet on the way home.

Your good friend,

I have no answer to a letter like this except a prayer of thanksgiving for the depth of spirit in my friend, and to hope that in some way I can continue to walk with him in his desert.

It is strange, if not embarrassing, to live the life of Nazareth in the heart of Jerusalem. It is an enigma to have a center of prayer, study and fraternal community in the midst of violence, injustice, despair and absurdity. The sense of powerlessness, helplessness can be overwhelming. The psalms of lamentation rise easily, of necessity, to one's lips:

> My heart quakes within me;
> the terror of death has fallen upon me.
> Fear and trembling come over me,
> and horror overwhelms me,—
>
> .   .   .
>
> for in the city I see violence and strife;
> day and night they prowl about upon its walls
> (Psalm 55).

Driving the freeway late at night, wearied and burdened with the undiminished problems of the day, I feel plunged back into the dark valleys of the Old Testament. "How long? Lord, how long!" As I drive over the intersection of the Ford and Lodge expressways, I am aware that it cuts a deep cross into the heart of the city. All day long hundreds of thousands crawl this way of the cross, each with their hidden or open crucifixion. How little the Gospel has penetrated. How few seem to believe, to understand. Within me the city cries out:

> I am worn out with groaning,
> every night I drench my pillow
> and soak my bed with tears;
> my eye is wasted with grief.
> I have grown old with enemies all around me.
> (Psalm 6).

The city is still the city of Isaias, the Suffering Servant. So little change has taken place. With darkened faith and hope I fall asleep.

Early in the morning I am awakened, mysteriously drawn to the Eucharist, for there is no other place to go. And I hear again, "Come, to the well and drink. Come, to the hearth and be warm. Come, to the table and eat. Come, to the Cross and understand. Stand under it!"

Yet his command persists: "Go, make disciples of all men, baptize. . .teach them to observe all the commandments I gave you." As I look over my city I feel much of the anguish which I felt one morning near Bombay on the shore of the Indian Ocean. Here I contemplated the six hundred million people living on that continent, waiting for the word of Christ. And I found myself asking, "How could You have begun such an impossible work! How could You have asked a dozen men to reshape the face of the earth, to recreate the heart of man!" His answer was quiet but uncompromising, unhesitant: "As the Father has sent me, I send you; as the Father has loved me, so I love you. And know that I am with you always; yes, to the end of time." The challenge is staggering, the good which any one person can do, rather insignificant. But it is to this challenge that we are called. In the words of Mother Theresa of Calcutta, "One drop changes the whole ocean, a person changes all mankind." Or in the words of Ghandi, "The love of one man is sufficient to compensate for the hatred of millions."

DISCIPLES AND OTHER STRANGERS

Over twenty years ago, Jerry Fraser, a classmate seminarian, and I took our first plunge into the inner city by doing a census of the Michigan Avenue skid row for Father Clem Kern of Holy Trinity Parish. We worked most of the summer in an effort to line up a contact person in each flop house for anyone who might need a priest. On the big evening for our first meeting with our thirty-three "committed" contact people, not one showed! Father Clem Kern tried to cheer us with words similar to the following: "Thank God for the experience. Prepare yourself and God will use you." The wisdom of these words has deepened within me over the years.

One summer during the early sixties I rented an apartment on Seward off Fourteenth Street where the riots of 1967 were later to break out. In this 101 unit apartment I spent a month knocking on doors, talking to the residents, trying to be friendly. What a strange phenomenon I must have been to them!—a white priest in an all-Black apartment. Not one of them had heard of St. Agnes Catholic Church a block and a half away. Even though, at first, most of them were suspicious that I might be an undercover policeman, they soon welcomed me with a warmth which went beyond the limits of politeness. I recall one man who opened his door with a paint brush in his hand. As he invited me in, he put it aside, remarking that he felt every man was worth an hour of his time.

I had several conversations with a man who had spent half his life in prison. He was now working with young people and commented that you find in people what you expect to find. If you are expecting the worst, they pick up your signal and give you the worst. If you are expecting their best, they will give you their best. You will find what you bring, what you are.

It did not take long to discover the anonymity of apartment people in the inner city. They learn fast and well that one does not trust anyone. No one knows his neighbor. No questions are asked, no answers are given. No hermits could have greater anonymity. But because of this isolation from one another, they can be easily victimized. One woman said that she would like to become a Catholic but knew she could not become one because of her previous marriage and her intention to marry again. "I cannot face *it* alone," was the way she expressed it. I asked her what she meant by "it". By her look, I knew she could not explain what she meant, for I had not experienced *it*. Slowly during those summer months and for the first time I began to understand that *"it"* was the real existence, presence and power of *Evil*. The city poor, through a real experience, had a sense of raw evil which I could never have, which I could only half believe in spite of "all my theology and scripture." "The mystery of iniquity is already at work" (2 Thess. 2,7). They had a keen perception that "evil" was at work, "taking over" certain people who then did violence and horrors which no human would be capable of doing alone. It was haunting to have some of them tell me that as long as I was there, "it" did not trouble them. But when I left, "it" returned.

As the summer drew to a close, I came to realize that I could spend the rest of my priesthood in this one apartment building and probably not be able to form it into a Christian community! This apartment was but 101 units. Within the one square mile area around me, there were 60,000 more units!

One can hold such thoughts on the threshold of consciousness only so long; and then they are erased by the new situations which break into one's life. After that summer I returned to my teaching at the seminary more sober, more humble about my capacity "to make disciples of all men." That summer I lost my "messiah complex" forever. Almost every week for the next year I went back to "our apartment" where we talked and prayed together. Before the next summer, the building was condemned, the people scattered again. Some still keep in contact. I never know when "Bill" or "Ramona" will surprise me with a call.

Before I became so involved in retreat and spiritual direction work, I used to spend a free afternoon in the "Cass Corridor" apartments near downtown, visiting door to door the retired welfare poor, barely eking out an existence. I simply spent a few moments talking to each as if they were old neighbors. Their faith, courage, heroism were great gifts to me. Indeed, in my moments with them, I felt a stranger in a strange land. I became a pilgrim with them. They shared with me their desert, welcomed me to their island. They taught me to pray.

This is the city of man. And as difficult as it is to believe that it is the City of God, it is, because he is here. He continues to pray over it, continues to weep, because I pray over it, because I weep over it—as much for myself as for those who sit in darkness and the shadow of death. I have always had a great desire to feel an enthusiastic civic spirit for my city, a great desire to make it into a new city which we could be "proud of." I am not optimistic; I am not pessimistic; neither am I mistic or mystic about it. But I do believe and I hear a loud voice calling:

You see this city? Here God lives among men. He will make his home among them; they shall be his people, and he will be their God; his name is God-with-them. He will wipe away all tears from their eyes, there will be no more death, and no more mourning or sadness. The world of the past has gone" (Rev. 21, 3).

IX CELTIC MEDITATIONS

Feet, Food, Darkness, Fire are the Great
Meditations of Holy Week. Liturgy is the
great teacher of prayer and in its cumulative experience is far wiser than many of
our other programs of instruction. A seri-
ous limitation of religious education in the
past has been to teach too much, too soon,
and then only in one dimension. This was
especially true in the area of prayer. We
were taught prayers long before we were
ready to pray, long before we discovered
what to pray about. We were taught con-
ceptually, given information, thoughts,
ideas about experiences which had not yet
happened for us. Prayer is wonder and
mystery, astonishment and excitement. It
is first-hand, primary, personal experience,
not derivative, second- or third-hand.
Prayer is experiential. There is nothing in
the mind, in the heart which is not first in
the body and senses. This is the basic
principle underlying the Incarnation, the
Liturgy, the Sacraments, the Church.

We cannot appreciate and enter deeply
into the Sacraments of Christ and the
Church unless we have experienced what is
sacred and holy in creation. "God saw all
he had made, and indeed it was very good"
(Gen. 1,31). There is much to unlearn and

much to learn for the first time. These exercises are intended as introductions, preludes, overtures, initiations into the great prayers of the Liturgy and Sacraments.

"Ever since God created the world his everlasting power and divinity—however invisible—have been there for the mind to see in the things he has made" (Romans 1,20).

"And he did this so that all nations might seek the Lord and, by *feeling their way* towards him, succeed in finding him" (Acts 17,27).

"Through Christ our Lord
You give us all these gifts.
You fill them with life and goodness
You bless them and make them holy"
(I Eucharistic Prayer).

"Everything exists within God" (Claudel).

"From the experiences of everyday things the mind and heart is lifted to him from whom all things flow. Everything is a gift of God's love, goodness, wonder and beauty. Everything can be a sacrament of God, an epiphany, a transparency of his presence. There is nothing in creation or man's experience that has not been an occasion of man's recognizing the power and presence of God. Our Lord took bread and wine, water and oil, human word and gesture and made of them encounters with himself" *(Surprised by the Spirit)*.

Many of God's gifts to us remain hidden and unseen simply because they are so near to us. He tells us again and again, "Unless you become like little children. . ."

Darkness

Fire

Food

even Feet

are invitations to pause and be drawn inward, to be caught and enchanted by the real beyond words and symbols, to experience the preludes to prayer and adoration.

MEDITATION   *Exercise in Faith,*
ON DARKNESS   *Prayer, Communion*
IN DARKNESS   *of Saints.*

Find yourself a room where there is total darkness, no cracks of light—a windowless room or auditorium, stage, storage room.

Seat yourself as comfortably as possible. Put out all the lights. Block out any cracks of light. Close your eyes, tune into your breathing, check your tension points, go into your deep center and be as totally quiet as possible.

Now open your eyes and experience the total darkness.

Be aware of your first feelings of the darkness. It is strange to open your eyes and to see nothing before you. In our contemporary culture filled with artificial light, total darkness is almost never experienced. We are deprived of the rich human experience of night. Most have lost the knowledge of stars, the mystery of twilight, of dawn. . .Light creates distance; darkness creates nearness and intimacy. Darkness removes space and time. All darkness is the same. This is the darkness that "covered the deep" in creation. This is the darkness that covered us in the womb, the darkness we knew as a child, the darkness which lies ahead of us in death and the tomb. . .When our eyes cannot function, the sense of touch intensifies. Be aware of the total alertness of your whole body. Be conscious of your body space, a delicate radar which extends beyond your body sensing what is close to you.

Now raise your hand and hold it in front of your face with your eyes wide open. . .You know it is there but you see nothing!

Darkness overcomes our self-consciousness; we may feel more free to speak.

Now feel free to express any feeling you are experiencing about the darkness. . .What must be the anguish of the person born blind. . .

Now as quietly as possible turn to the person on either side and look into their face. . .You know they are there but you look into nothing! or they may be looking the other way!

(If there is adequate space and no obstacles to run into or trip over)—

As quietly as possible stand up and begin very slowly and gently to move around the room. If you feel nervous and want to laugh, let yourself breathe deeply and return to your peace center. You will feel others brush by you as you move by them. This is what we do all the time, especially with those we know...Now sit down again wherever you are, and reflect upon this experience of walking in the darkness, not knowing who walks with you.

We think of God as Light, but God is also Darkness. Often in darkness we can sense him more near than in the light. Light creates distance; darkness, closeness and intimacy. As darkness encompasses me completely, so does God. "No one has ever seen God, it is the only Son, who is nearest to the Father's heart, who has made him known." Only faith can overcome the darkness which envelopes our mind and reason. In the darkness we cannot see our hand an inch before our eyes nor the face which is next to our own. Wonderful are our eyes, but how little they "see." They catch only the light reflected from another surface. In darkness we "see" so much more deeply. In daylight we hardly recognize a face at fifty feet; at night we can see the distant galaxy!

Who was that who passed you in the dark, the one you brushed against with your left shoulder? It could have been anyone. It could have been him! It was! It is!

Your eyes tell you that there is no one in the room. Yet you know it is filled with people. You cannot see prayer but whenever you pray you know that you are connected with everyone who prays. Whenever one prays he is in Christ and Christ is in him and with him is the communion and community of saints—"That they may be one as we are one. With me in them and you in me" (John 17,22).

Now close your eyes as the lights are turned on. Begin to share your experience with the person you find next to you.

MEDITATION ON   *Exercise on*
FOOD   *Eucharist and*
                         Community

Eating in all world religions is a holy and sacred action. One of the oldest, longest retained of religious customs is the one of praying before and after meals. Food Prayers are our most consistent act of thanksgiving (or complaint!—Lament Psalms are not uncommon in the prayer of the Hebrew Scriptures). Until the mid-fifties, in most religious communities and seminaries, meals were eaten in silence accompanied by spiritual reading. This remains the practice in some monastic communities.

It is not surprising that this tradition of so many centuries became extinct almost over night. People forget. The language of a tradition is no longer understood. The practice is discarded. But deep human values and truths do not remain buried for long. One discovers the "new" only to realize later that it is as old, as young as humanity itself.

In Japan and India, I rediscovered the ancient value of the silent meal and the meditation of food. The tea ceremony of the Japanese is a contemplative action which comes close to the reverence, depth, simplicity of a Trappist Liturgy. The prayers before meals in a Buddhist monastery are twice as long as the time for consuming one's food in silence. Before a Hindu eats his food he first places it before the altar and in prayer offers it to the deity. Viewing this immediately recalled to my memory the Old Testament "peace offerings," the sacrifice of communion, a meal of joy in which the best portion was offered, burnt for the Lord, the rest eaten by the offerers. Thus the idea of food prolonging the ritual sacrifice and communion with God.

All food is "manna" from God. All eating can be a communion with him, the Giver, the Lover of all. Our food is not blessed in the quick sign of the cross or the too-hurried words of "grace." The sign, the words do not make the meal holy. They are but a recognition of the truth that the action one is about to perform *is* already holy. Grace is an act of reverence before that which is holy, a gift from him who is All Holy. Prayer is a recognition that he who eats is holy, is son of God, son of his Father, anticipating the heavenly banquet.

Let us begin.

Everyone is seated at the dinner table. This meditation will be best appreciated if the meal is a Sunday or festive one; and if everyone as well as the table is "dressed" for the occasion. We do too much "eating," too little "dining." No prayer is "recited." The act of our eating will be our prayer.

Close your eyes, tune into your breathing, check your tension points, go into your peace center and begin to relish what you are about to eat. Begin to welcome your "manna" with a joyful, thankful smile.

Open your eyes and let your eyes "feast" on what you are about to eat. Use your silverware or be free to use your fingers. Little children know how to enjoy their food; they usually play with it for a while.

Savour whatever you eat as long as you can. Let it liquify before you swallow it. Be aware that this is a holy act, so holy that Jesus uses it as the occasion for performing his miracle, giving us his deepest words, leaving us forever his Body and Blood as our food and drink.

Listen to your food, let it speak its word, its secret, its history to you. Enjoy the color, the texture, the size, shape, the sound. All the world is present upon your table. How many unseen hands have labored to fill your plate!

What you are eating is letting go of its life in order to enter into your life. Now the food becomes you. Family table. . .Father's house. Mother's flour, Father's grapes. . . bread—creation of women's hand. . .wine— work of man's hands. "Give us this day our daily bread." God so loved the world that he became food, our bread and wine. He changes bread and wine into himself. . .So are we to become what he is. We change bread and wine into our body and blood. When we eat his Body and drink his Blood, he changes us into himself. "I live, no longer I, but Christ lives in me."

Sharing the same table is the sign of friendship, of love, of sharing the same life. To eat together is to receive one another. . .

When the Body and Blood of Christ is rendered present, we who are the whole Christ are rendered present. When we receive him, we receive all who are one in him.

"If you love me, *feed* my sheep."

When you have finished eating, close your eyes and remain in your center; be aware that when your eating is finished, the processing of your body is but begun. Be aware of the mystery of your new life unfolding.

Now open your eyes and share your thanksgiving with one another.

MEDITATION	Exercise of the
ON WASHING	*"Sign of*
OF FEET	*Discipleship"*

This is a meditation exercise taught by Christ himself. The whole Christian Community is invited to experience and celebrate this "sign" in the solemn Liturgy of Holy Thursday. It is a sign that some of the early Fathers of the Church looked upon as a Sacrament. Many have watched this ceremony from the edge of the crowd; few have participated in this liturgical experience directly, even though we are each under his command, "If I, then, your Lord and Master, have washed your feet, you should wash each other's feet!" This is a very awkward and embarrassing command. We can readily identify with Peter and cry out, "Never! You shall never wash my feet." But in the next breath we are confronted with the awesome response of Jesus to Peter: "If I do not wash you, you can have nothing in common with me!"

This exercise is best celebrated with a family-size group in the setting of the Eucharistic Liturgy, as Christ himself celebrated it.

Everyone comes with bare feet.

Let the group be seated in a circle, or circles, with a basin, pitcher and towels in the center. The Liturgy of the Word is that of Holy Thursday. Each one prays silently for a

deep spirit of prayer and humility to overcome the natural nervousness and reluctance
before such an experience.

The priest reads the Gospel of John, Chapter
13, 1-11: "It was before the festival of the
Passover. . .(Jerusalem translation). . .though
not all of you are." Here the priest pauses,
takes off his chasuble and stole, and takes
the basin, pitcher and towel to the person on
his right.

Let everyone close his eyes, tune into his
breathing, go into his deep center to experience fully the mystery and symbolism of
this action of Christ which he is about to
have done to him and which he will do to
another.

The priest with prayer and reverence washes both
feet of the person before whom he kneels.
As he dries each foot, he kisses it in an act of
humility. Then the priest gives the towel and
water to the person whose feet he has just
washed and that person in turn washes the
feet of the next person in the same manner.
This continues around, with the last person
in the circle washing the feet of the priest.

No music or singing is necessary. Let each
person be in prayer, listen to the sounds of
the washing and remember that Last Supper.
Before he took bread into his hands, he took
the feet of his disciples!

When the priest's feet have been washed, he
puts on his vestments and continues the
Gospel of John 13, 12-18: "When he had
washed their feet and put on his clothes

again he went back to the table. Do you understand. . .Now that you know this, happiness will be yours if you behave accordingly."

Let us meditate. . .

"Do *you* understand what *I* have done to you?" Who washed your feet? It could have been anyone's hands. . .It could have been his!. . .It was! He has no other hands! Whose feet did you wash? It could have been anyone's feet. It could have been his feet!. . .It was! He has no other feet! He has no other hands, no other feet, except yours and mine!

Before he took bread into his hands to change it into his body, he first took the feet of his disciples! What an "anointing" that must have been! And how necessary, if these feet were ever to follow in his footsteps. "How beautiful are the feet of those who carry the glad tidings of the Good News" (Isaiah). Could they ever forget the way in which he held, washed and kissed their feet! What strength they must have drawn from the remembrance of that moment, when at other moments their feet were weary and bleeding from the hard roads of their missionary journeys.

One wonders about his hands and feet. What were they like, those hands and feet which were to be nailed to the cross before the sun set the next day!

How blessed are the feet of those who follow him! Now it is the touch of our feet which makes the ground holy. Take off your shoes and the earth becomes holy! Follow Me, follow My footprints, the path which My feet have created, and for which your feet have now been annointed.

Now share your response with your community.

The community then "footprints" its way to the Eucharistic Table to continue the Liturgy.

MEDITATION
ON FIRE

Meditation on fire is the first of the meditations which the Church teaches us in the Liturgy of the Easter Vigil. But this is too rich a meditation to be limited to one night. Every sanctuary lamp, every candle enkindled on the altar is an invitation to remember, to re-celebrate the mystery, the sacrament, the prayer of fire.

Gather the group around the fireplace or the bonfire in the open air.

Declare the silence and invite each one to watch for the spark or flame which ignites the fire. The wonder of a spark struck from flint, fire leaping from a stone!

No directed relaxation is necessary. Fire itself quiets and moves one into the deeper silences within.

The taming of fire was man's first conquest, the Prometheus stealing fire from the gods. Fire is man's oldest ally, never irreversibly a friend, too easily an enemy. Fire is never totally domesticated; it owns itself, retaining its unpredictable wildness and destructiveness. It can be controlled but not changed. Whatever it touches, it turns into itself. Yet it cannot exist by itself; it must adhere, inhere to something. Fire is transformative; it creates something new, shapes old things into ever new possibilities. Fire is man's great servant, his most powerful and creative tool. Man cannot touch fire, yet learning to harness it has given him his civilization. The story of civilization and culture is the story of fire from hearth to outer space, from flint spark to atomic bomb.

Now let each one speak aloud his stream of consciousness which the fire draws out of him: Poetry, song, prayer, Scripture.

"I have come to cast fire on the earth and I would that it be enkindled."

"And something appeared to them that seemed like tongues of fire; these separated and came to rest on the head of each of them."

"...to Jesus heart all burning with fervent love for men."

Pillar of fire by night.

"With a live coal he touched my mouth" (Isaiah 6,6).